WAYMARKS

*Signposts to discovering
God's presence in the world*

Peter Millar

CANTERBURY
PRESS
Norwich

For the villagers of South India
who taught me so much.

© Peter W. Millar 2000

First published in 2000 by
The Canterbury Press Norwich
(a publishing imprint of Hymns Ancient & Modern Limited
a registered charity)
St Mary's Works, St Mary's Plain
Norwich, Norfolk, NR3 3BH

British Library Cataloguing in Publication Data

A catalogue record for this book is available
from the British Library

ISBN 1-85311-336-0

Typeset by Regent Typesetting, London
and printed in Great Britain by
Biddles Ltd, Guildford and King's Lynn

Contents

Contents

Contents

Introduction

God so loved the world, she got involved

Church poster

Set up waymarks for yourself,
make yourself guideposts:
consider well the highway,
the road by which you went.

Jeremiah 31:21

Sheltered by the mountains and close to Scotland's River Spey is the small village of Laggan in southern Inverness-shire. Like many Highland communities it carries an ancient history: the lives and struggles of successive generations who despite the harsh climate have worked the land, fished the rivers, planted the forests and made of it a green place.

In recent years, some of the Laggan villagers have taken over the management of three thousand acres of surrounding forest land. It is a scheme which is bringing employment and fresh hope to the local people. One part of this project is the construction of new paths amidst the larch and pine forests. One of these tracks leads to a small ruined village which was last inhabited around a century ago. In time, it is hoped that one of the traditional cottages there will be restored – reminding future generations of that amazingly rich story, marked by poverty and determination, of their Highland forbears, many of whom walked with God.

It is not easy for the visitor to find this hidden village, and by the side of the path leading to it various waymarks, usually huge stones dug from the soil, have been placed. They not only signify the correct route, but also remind the walker that there is still some way to go! Without these obvious waymarks, that beautiful path through the woods would be incomplete. It needs the signposts just to occasionally remind us that we are on the right track. Although obvious, they are not intrusive. They announce themselves in a quiet way, although their message is unmistakable. They point us to the next stage on our journey.

So it is with the spiritual waymarks which I write about in this book. In themselves they may be fragmentary, incomplete and hedged about with all kinds of limitations, yet they are intended to point us forward, opening up new possibilities for our journey with God. And they arise from my own journey as a Christian person who has many questions, inner contradictions, uncertainties and also faith in God, however fragile.

My wife Dorothy and I have had the privilege of working in many parts of the world. For a long time we lived in south India with our children, and experienced first-hand the treasures of another culture. That complex and wonderful country taught us a basic truth – that we are all pilgrims and seekers; often restless wanderers like the people of Israel. We have no continuing address on this earth, even when we spend much of our energy in the search for security and rootedness. Within our lives, we keep moving, emotionally and spiritually, even if we have lived in the same home for sixty years!

Yet however fragile our faith may be, and however restless our hearts, in the pages of the Bible we meet a God who loves this world and the people in it. There is always a dialogue going on between the Creator and the created. At one level we know very little about the mystery of God and of his or her purposes on earth, yet what is revealed is a life-giving waymark to which we can return again and again. That is what makes our earthly pilgrimage so exciting, bewildering and surprising.

In the Old Testament, that extraordinary person, the prophet Jeremiah, looks forward to that day when the exiled people of Israel will return home. In this bleak wilderness of exile, God finds his people and rescues them; from the far corners of the earth come the blind, broken and obstinate to the outstretched hands of God. At the time of his writings, the exiles have not yet reached the point of return, but their homecoming has been assured which is why mourning can take flight and the streets be filled with dancing. God will respond to their prayers and, with penitent and joyful hearts, the exiles can walk the final miles. Tears are dried away and bruised spirits are made whole again.

In these circumstances, the exiles are invited by God to set their sights on the highway and erect their waymarks. These need to be authentic lest the people lose sight of that central vision which is grounded in their Creator's justice, wisdom, love and healing. Significant in themselves, the waymarks also point beyond – opening windows of vision and insight for the pilgrims, even in their present suffering. They are symbols of that which is yet to be, disclosing many truths.

This ever-moving God not only makes sacred our human story, but sings through all creation, and in the natural order many of God's waymarks are apparent. This to me is a fundamental truth as we seek for spiritual waymarks in the coming years, and in that sense much of what I write is about our essential connectedness – to God, to one another and to the good earth itself.

Although my Christian journey has been full of pot-holes, false turnings and mind-blowing contradictions, I am powerfully attracted to the message of the Gospels and the person of Christ. My understanding of Jesus was immeasurably deepened by my contacts with Hinduism in India, and by the knowledge of God which is held within so many Indian hearts. While I may be uncomfortable with traditional religious language, I profoundly believe that in giving oneself to Jesus Christ, we embark on a journey towards wholeness. A friend in India, the late Bede Griffiths, a Benedictine monk who was a spiritual mentor to many people, used to speak about the 'marriage of East and West' in his own soul; a marriage which enlarged his love for Christ and his understanding of Christianity.

Threading through the waymarks which are mentioned in this book is my conviction that the western world, given its present state of fragmentation, cannot save itself. If healing is to take place, as God intends it should, we must listen to the voices inherent in different cultures and in religious traditions other than our own. To do that is not to throw overboard these great and life-giving waymarks which are at the heart of the Christian message, but to be awakened to the truth that they are so much broader and deeper than we can ever imagine. As St Paul said with typical eloquence in his letter to the small group of Christians in Ephesus:

Introduction

> To him who by means of his power working in us is able
> to do so much more than we can ever ask for, or even
> think of: to God be the glory in the church and in Christ
> Jesus for all time, for ever and ever! Amen.
>
> *Ephesians 3:20–21*

And while I am convinced that the natural order is in itself
sacred and speaks of God's glory, I also believe that the
people around me, who like myself stumble and fall and get
up again, also reveal that divine image. That's why some of
their stories run through these pages; they are truly waymarks for our times. The laughter and agony of ordinary
lives, often lived out in circumstances of violence and
poverty, are contemporary signposts of extraordinary
moment. These are God's almost incredible stories: anger-
making, passion-rousing, poetic, reassuring, healing and
faith-filled. Waymarks all, if we only take the time to listen!

A book such as this is not meant to be read through from
cover to cover – which is perhaps a statement of the obvious!
If some of my reflections can start you off on a new path-
way, that will be great. You don't need to 'agree' with what
I've written, and you may disagree with the whole book,
but at least recognize in yourself why that be the case!

One Friday evening several years ago, as I sat in a corner
in one of the ancient temples in south India and watched
something like thirty thousand women, children and men
pass by me on their way to prayer, I knew God was a far,
far greater reality than anything I could imagine. But in
that sacred place which has held the prayers of millions
through thousands of years, I also recognized that the 'still
small voice' within me was God's. My Celtic forbears, who
saw themselves as pilgrims, would instantly know that

intuitive recognition. God within – always in tenderness calling us home; the image of God resting deep within our lives, however halting our faith.

A huge part of me believes in a God who today weeps over our frenzied attempts at personal accumulation, our despoiling of the earth and our apparent self-absorption in a global village where millions starve. I don't think I have ever been comfortable with a God who is only located in the churches, and I feel at home with those who in their search for God often stumble and fall. The waymarks about which I have written in these pages spring from a heart which knows inner confusion and rich blessing in equal measure. And as my friends know well, I can easily understand folk who want to climb a mountain in the rain at midnight or keep telling the most stupid jokes! It's all part and parcel of God's amazing love for us all in a world threaded through with unexpected, life-giving possibilities.

> Lord of every new day
> when the road ahead is
> totally scary
> or far too comfortable,
> reveal your
> life-giving waymarks,
> so that having made them our own,
> we travel on with
> risk,
> vulnerability,
> vision,
> awareness,
> passion,
> struggle,

energy
and compassion
as our constant companions.

Suggestions for using this book

* the book is not intended to be read straight through from cover to cover

* each waymark or theme stands on its own, although a connecting thread runs through them all

* underlying the various waymarks is the conviction that God is to be found in the midst of ordinary life and in the natural world, and that the Bible invites us to live out an engaged, radical faith journey with the help of the Spirit

* a single waymark may provide a starting point for Biblical reflection or prayer or meditation, or all three

* a small group may use a waymark or several of them as a way into discussion or shared prayer

* a waymark may suggest ways in which individuals or groups can be more directly involved with local and global issues

* the books suggested for further reading enlarge on many of the themes raised in the various waymarks.

I

Seeking

As a deer longs for a stream of cool water, so I long for God.

Psalm 42:1

Returning to God is a life-long journey.

Henri Nouwen[1]

Every day is a messenger of God.

Russian Proverb

We have believed that beautiful flowers grow out of pure elements. In fact, as the lotus reminds us, their roots go down into every sort of impurity and rottenness. Thus our spiritual quest must proceed not by means of separation, of walking out on ourselves, but rather by staying on and going deeper.

Angela West[2]

It's OK to be a seeker! That's the thread that runs through these pages and I hope that the various waymarks which I write about help you to be more confident in your own search for truth, for meaning, for insight, for God. Returning 'home', in the sense of discovering that God walks with us on the journey, takes a life-time. Wisdom is not going to come in one minute! Yet so long as we are willing to take risks, be open, work for justice, love the earth, reach out to our neighbour and travel within, we shall discern many waymarks – often some truly amazing ones.

Kenneth Leech, who is both an Anglican priest and a prophet for our times, speaks of 'the energy derived from yearning'. I think that is a wonderful phrase – affirming, challenging – and one from which all seekers can find inspiration. It is God's energy that lies within our yearning. It is part of our human condition to have restless hearts – but it is these often contradictory journeys of the soul which connect us to the One who created us. It is not possible to have a static spirit. The Danish writer, Søren Kierkegaard, put that truth succinctly when he wrote that 'we are always *becoming* people of faith'. In other words, life is a pilgrimage: a movement into God who pervades the whole of creation.

And our search for God's wisdom takes place amidst the ordinary experiences of life: within our fragmented lives which run in several directions at the same time. I believe that profoundly, which is why this poem finds its roots in the fluctuations and bewilderments of my own existence. They are the words of a 'seeker after truth' who believes in a God who never answers all our questions, but understands far more clearly that we do, where they come from.

> Am I alone in yearning for
> the recovery of vision,
> of authentic outrage,
> of gentle connectedness,
> of the truth that sets us free?
>
> Do you tell me that such
> idealism is impossible
> in a world of junk mail,

easy money,
fleeting icons,
fragile relationships
and grinding poverty?

With you I ask,
can the miracle of God's light
permeate
all this?

Can we still hear
that single voice of Love
through these myriad cries,
or see in our neighbour
the face of God?

Can the angels
stop us in our tracks
as we relentlessly
seek life elsewhere?

My friend,
in our shared uncertainty
we stand with our peoples,
broken like them;
but also, with them –
propelled still
to befriend
the amazing and unpredictable
wisdom of God.

2

Wonder

Whoever is devoid of the capacity to wonder, whoever remains unmoved, whoever cannot contemplate or know the deep shudder of the soul in enchantment, might just as well be dead for he has already closed his eyes upon life.

Albert Einstein

Centuries ago, St Augustine made the observation that the human mind has the capacity not only to observe, measure and explore creation, but also the ability to wonder at it. Spontaneous wonder. Often on a gloriously clear night, I look up at the heavens and remember that the nearest fixed star I see is about 25 million miles away. Close to that twinkling light are hundreds of others making it almost impossible to believe a former Astronomer Royal when he calculated that six specs of dust in Waterloo Station represent the extent to which space is populated with stars (but I do trust his calculation, standing in awe at his knowledge of the universe).

The Milky Way, which Michael Mayne, the former Dean of Westminster, described as part of our local neighbourhood in terms of space, is only one of a vast assemblage of galaxies (taking some two million years for light to get from one to the next) and it contains about 300 thousand million stars. And the multiple galaxies beyond the Milky Way are receding away from us in a continually expanding creation. As Michael pointed out: 'No longer can we say "Twinkle, twinkle little star, how I wonder what you are!" for we know they shine because they are furnaces of raging gas, mainly hydrogen and helium, held together by gravity but not lasting for ever.'[1]

And spontaneous wonder takes over when we realize that our imagination alone cannot conceive of this scale of reality. We stand in awe. We are silent. We celebrate the unfolding of creation. And in these spontaneous moments of wonder, sometimes a prayer is born. A prayer framed in human words but with an internal movement which transcends them.

Here is such a prayer from George MacLeod: words conceived in wonder and pointing beyond our limited categories of definition.

> Once more we give thanks,
> for earth and sea and sky in harmony of colour,
> the air of the eternal seeping through the physical,
> the everlasting glory dipping into time.
> For nature resplendent;
> growing beasts, mergent crops, singing birds,
> We bless Thee.
>
> For swift running tides,
> resistant waves,
> Thy spirit on the waters:
> O Lord: how marvellous are Thy works
> In majesty hast Thou created them.
>
> *George MacLeod*[2]

This deep shudder of the soul in enchantment is something we cannot live without. We all desperately need those moments of interruption which bring our life to a standstill as sheer wonder fills our being – those times when we feel held within cosmic currents and flows. And in such moments of wonder we are addressed by our Creator: summoned by the still small whisper of God. Chief Dan George speaks of this from the wisdom of his Native American tradition:

> The beauty of the trees,
> the softness of the air,
> the fragrance of the grass,
> speaks to me.
>
> The summit of the mountain,
> the thunder of the sky,
> the rhythm of the sea,
> speaks to me.
>
> The faintness of the stars,
> the freshness of the morning,
> the dewdrop on the flower,
> speaks to me.
>
> The strength of fire,
> the taste of salmon,
> the trail of the sun,
> and the life that never goes away,
> they speak to me.
>
> And my heart soars.[3]

Our soaring hearts, held in wonder. And maybe we need the quiet wisdom of a child to experience such enchantment. On the porch of our church in the East End of Glasgow there hung a poster. It had on it a simple message: 'Let go; let God.' When I come to think about it, it is often when we can 'let go', even momentarily, of our inner baggage, that these shafts of wonder unexpectedly announce themselves, and in doing so disclose new horizons.

The famous cellist, Pablo Casals, never lost his sense of wonder, and at the age of 93 could write:

> For the past eighty years I have started each day in the same manner. I go to the piano, and I play two preludes and fugues of Bach. It is a sort of benediction on the house. But that is not its only meaning. It is a rediscovery of the world in which I have the joy of being a part. It fills me with awareness of the wonder of life, with a feeling of the incredible marvel of being human.[4]

Rediscovering the wonder of it all, and moving into a deeper awareness of our own humanity, is a fundamental stage on our spiritual journey. The Ashanti people in West Africa have known that for centuries, which is why they can write prayers which enlarge our often limited horizons.

> O God,
> creator of our land,
> our earth, the trees,
> the animals and humans,
> all is for your honour.
>
> The drums beat it out,
> and people sing about it,
> and they dance with noisy joy
> that you are Lord.

You have also pulled the other continents
out of the sea.
What a wonderful world you have made
out of wet mud,
and what beautiful men and women!
We thank you for all the beauty of this earth.

The grace of your creation is like a cool day
between rainy seasons.
We drink your creation with our eyes.
We listen to the birds' jubilee
with our ears.

How strong and good
and sure your earth smells,
and everything that grows there.
Bless us.
Bless our land and people.
Bless our forests with mahogany,
wawa, and cacao.
Bless our fields with cassava and peanuts.
Bless the waters
that flow through our land.

Fill them with fish
and drive great schools of fish to our seacoast,
so that the fishermen in their unsteady boats
do not need to go out too far.

Be with us in our countries
and in all Africa,
and in the whole world.
Prepare us for the service that we should render.

Ashanti Prayer[5]

3

Reawakening to mystery

Apprehend God in all things,
for God is in all things.

Every single creature is full of God
and is a book about God.

Every creature is a word of God.

If I spent enough time with the tiniest creature –
even a caterpillar –
I would never have to prepare a sermon.
So full of God is every creature.

Meister Eckhart

Grandfather Great Spirit
All over the world the faces of living ones are alike.
With tenderness they have come up out of the ground.
Look upon your children that they may face the winds
   and walk the good road to the Day of Quiet.
Grandfather Great Spirit
Fill us with the Light.
Give us the strength to understand,
   and the eyes to see.
Teach us to walk the soft Earth as relatives
   to all that live.

Sioux Prayer

The prophetic writings of the American Charlene Spetnak carry a compelling invitation to us all to awaken to that sense of the mystery which lies deep within every human being. Her book, *States of Grace*, propels us to rediscover and to reconnect with the sacred whole. In my opinion, her work brings us back to understand ourselves more deeply, to discern with greater clarity and focus the times in which we live, and underlines the intricate mysteries of existence. It shows that a 'sense of mystery' is central to a meaningful life, and not an escape from it; a source of healing threading through everyday life.

Yet how do we recover this consciousness of mystery when we have grown up in a culture which is essentially hostile to anything which cannot be proved by science?

One of the facts of life on the island of Iona is that each day one comes face to face with the elements; rain, wind, sunshine, thunderstorms and rainbows. It was the same for Columba and his monks over fourteen hundred years ago, and in a thousand or fifty thousand years from now, these elemental forces will still sweep across the remote beaches and gentle hills of the Hebridean isle. It is not surprising that many regard Iona as 'a thin place' between the material and spiritual dimensions of life.

But for most of us, our lives are in the thick of the city, within concrete and steel landscapes far from sea-girt islands. We do not see space as 'sacred' and are often violently disconnected from the natural order and from that pervasive sense of intimacy with it which character-ized the lives of our forbears. Amidst the mind-blowing achievements and certainties of technology it is not difficult to lose our sense of mystery.

In the nineteenth century, Chief Seattle warned that humans would die of terrible loneliness if all the animals disappeared, yet how many of us even notice the gradual disappearance of songbirds, for instance, as fewer return each spring from their ravished homes in various parts of the globe? The diminishing bird counts are items we read about in the newspaper and then turn the page. Is it us who are dying, slowly but surely, of terrible alienation? Unable to be in touch with that finely balanced relatedness between humans and the earth in all of its amazing vitality and complexity?

Within my own life, an awakening consciousness to mystery has been a long learning curve. Like everyone else in the western world, I have been influenced and shaped by a mechanistic approach to life and in such a climate the rediscovery of 'the sacred whole' does not happen overnight. The Christianity which I was brought up with tended to sacralize the human story (and the human story is sacred) and separate it from a larger reality. It was only after I went to live in India which, by and large, has not lost this interconnectedness with a wider canvas, that I awoke to the spiritual poverty attached to the view which makes only our human journey sacred.

For some Christians, this awakening to a sense of mystery at the heart of life, raises all kinds of alarm bells. They are fearful that in touching into the natural order which gives birth to mystery, we are in danger of losing Christ and his message of forgiveness. They believe that in celebrating and rejoicing in the natural order, we are failing to take seriously human evil; that we are moving away from the truths of the gospel into an ill-defined spirituality. That human failures all become relative, and that, in the end, everything is acceptable.

As an individual totally committed to the truths of the Christian faith, I answer these critical voices by saying that in the Western Church we have too readily domesticated the gospel. We sometimes worship a 'small God' and not the One who holds the universe in his hands. One parishioner when asked by her vicar if she believed in a God who held heaven and earth, who healed, transformed, liberated and renewed creation, paused for a moment. Then she replied: 'No, I don't. I believe in the ordinary God.' The 'ordinary God' is so often only a god of our own devising.

The writers of the Old Testament lived with the knowledge that humanity had always been faced with the divine mystery. From the very beginning, human beings had been in the presence of mystery – the mystery of existence which they explored. Hebrew religion springs from this encounter with the sacred mystery.

In Hebrew the word for sacred mystery is 'elohim', a plural form which originally must have meant 'the gods'. It was a word signifying the whole world of the gods, that is the sacred mystery itself. With the coming of Abraham, the founder of the people of Israel, came the experience of a transcendent God who manifested himself in the history of a particular people. But it was through the symbols of mystery, such as flaming fire, that Abraham received God's revelation. It was the same with the prophets: God revealed, through water, cloud, fire and thunder.

In the New Testament, St Paul speaks of the body as the 'temple of the Holy Spirit' and this is itself a mystery which our fragile words cannot ever adequately express. What does it mean when we say that the divine energy of Christ's love is flowing through our lives? We may experience this but it is not possible to give it definition. Over the centuries, hundreds of books have been written about the Holy Spirit in the lives of individuals, but it remains a sacred mystery as to why in the first place our human condition should be permeated with the divine. God's wisdom is beyond our imagining, and we lightly tread on a planet whose complexities, as present scientific work affirms, are much, much greater than could ever be visualised by the human mind.

When the Orthodox Church met in conference some years ago, in Bulgaria, this statement was issued. For me, it brings home an image of a God in whom everything is held, human and non-human, the whole creation witnessing to the Creator's love.

> As the Orthodox Church, we need to find ways to support sound programmes which seek to preserve from pollution air, water and land. To speak of the re-integration of creation today is first to speak words of repentance and to make commitments towards the new way of living for the whole of humanity. The contemporary world must repent for the abuses which we have imposed on the natural world. The human race thinks that it can make arbitrary use of the earth, as though earth did not have its own requisites and a prior God-given purpose, which people must not betray. Instead of carrying out its role as a co-operator with God in the work of creation, humanity sets itself up in place of God and thus ends by provoking a rebellion on the part of nature.[1]

As we begin to listen again to what the Orthodox Church calls 'the earth's own requisites and God-given purpose', we reawaken to the sense of mystery deep in ourselves. We realise that all things in creation interconnect; that we are indeed part of a sacred whole, a sacred mystery. And in this movement of consciousness we start to experience an inner feeling of thankfulness to God for giving the gift of this hugely intricate web of inter-relatedness.

For a thousand generations, human beings viewed themselves as part of this wider community of nature, and they carried on active relationships not only with other people, but with other animals, plants, and natural objects including mountains, rivers, winds and weather patterns. Human beings knew that they belonged and were 'at home' in this wider frame of meaning, as is so evident from the prayers of my own Celtic forbears.

For many of us today, this journey into the rediscovery of mystery is essentially a 'journey home' – into our fuller identity as God's people. It is not a running-away from the realities of the contemporary world; nor is it some elitist concern. I believe it is the opposite. It is a coming to terms with the basic fact that our lives must be earthed in a humble acceptance that we travel on this earth lightly and provisionally; that we have no permanent resting place; that God holds out to us grace-filled moments when we simply 'stand in awe' and are silent at the wonder of it all.

Reawakening to mystery; returning home and finding ourselves at one with God's vast and interdependent universe; seeking the humility, grace and tenderness that comes from being fully a part of that incredibly diverse sacred whole. A truth illustrated in some lyrical words by David Abram:

An alder leaf, loosened by wind, is drifting out with the tide. As it drifts, it bumps into the slender leg of a great blue heron staring intently through the rippled surface, then drifts on. The heron raises one leg out of the water and replaces it, a single step. As I watch I, too, am drawn into the spread of silence. Slowly, a bank of cloud approaches, slipping its bulged and billowing texture over the earth, folding the heron and the alder trees and

my gazing body into the depths of a vast breathing being,
enfolding us all within a common flesh, a common story
now bursting with rain.

David Abram[2]

Enfolded in a common story, a common flesh. These moving words mirror a 'personal creed' which a friend has
given to me. It is Jenny's own waymark, disclosing in poetic language a fragment of this vast mystery of which we are
a tiny part.

I believe in

    – the awesome underlying simplicity
                     complexity
                     variety
   of the natural world.

    – a delicate balance of opposites
          order and disorder
          freedom and strict laws
          randomness and determined outcomes
          deep patterns; deep harmony.

    – the prolific outpouring of natural energy,
       the cycling of resource
       the abundant fertility and nurturing
       the ability to adapt with wondrous ingenuity
           evolving to uniqueness and interdependence
               in fine tension.

– the intrinsic beauty, value and potential
    of every part of the natural world,
      living and non-living,
    and of each individual life.

– the otherness of the human being
    its protective system of pain
    its healing powers
    its senses and perceptions
    pleasure
    colour
    music.

– earthly life as set in a context
    free of time and space.

– existence and reality beyond.

1. Mon 19 8:44pm
   Ron

2. Mon 19 8.49
   Betty

3. Wed 24th 3.59
   Mary CB

4. Fri 11.34
   or
   Kingfisher

earth

aters

ranates,

without scarcity,

ine copper.

You shall eat your fill
and bless the LORD your God
for the good land
he has given you.

Deuteronomy 8:7–11

Only after the last tree has been cut down;
Only after the last river has been poisoned;

Only after the last fish has been caught;
Only then will you find that money cannot be eaten.

Cree Indian Prophecy

It is happening! Slowly we are awakening from our slumber and listening to the cries of our wounded earth. No longer are environmental issues of marginal interest. If we are to survive as a species, we have no alternative but to befriend the glorious and unfolding natural world of which we are a tiny part. As we move into a new millennium, the idea that the earth needs friends to feel, think and act on its behalf, has touched and moved people all over the world.

That wonderful poem from West Africa, from the Yoruba peoples, speaks to us with immediate relevance:

> Enjoy the earth gently,
> enjoy the earth gently;
> for if the earth is spoiled
> it cannot be repaired.
> Enjoy the earth gently.

For centuries, many Christians presumed that God's love was primarily directed at them, and that the natural order was created mainly for the use, and abuse, of mankind. Robert Runcie, who in my estimation was a great Archbishop of Canterbury, pointed out that such a human-centred attitude to our fragile and exhausted planet is at last beginning to look not only selfish and parochial, but also irresponsible and potentially dangerous.

All of us need an enlarged vision in our understanding of the environment. Surely, in the years ahead, we must realize that the way to maintain the value and preciousness of the human is by reaffirming the sacredness of the non-human also – of all that is. As the Psalmist said: 'O LORD, our Lord, your greatness is seen in all the world' (Psalm 8:1). This is not a description of a dispensable universe, but of one fashioned in love by the Creator. And nothing that is fashioned in such a way can ever be regarded as of secondary importance.

I recently had the privilege of interviewing many people who are involved in environmental concerns. One of them was a friend called Leslie who, with his wife Sheila, runs a small croft in a very beautiful part of Inverness-shire. Leslie was brought up on a socially disadvantaged housing estate in the Midlands, but when he was a young child he began to observe small living creatures such as lizards and newts on a piece of wasteground behind his home. From these childhood memories has sprung an extraordinary commitment in his life to work on behalf of the earth: to befriend it with gentle understanding and grace.

Leslie's poems keep re-shaping the way I look at nature, and for this I am grateful. Here, in a piece entitled 'Edge of the Wood', Leslie evokes something of the quiet mystery inherent in the natural order which surrounds us.

> No shell or echo
> Could sound such darkness;
> No valley below
> A mountain's vastness
> Could house such loneliness.
> Not a sound was heard
> Above the river's flood –
> Man nor beast stirred
> In the morning wood.
> Only the wind understood.
>
> *Leslie Bates*[1]

As we re-learn how to walk in gentle solidarity with the earth, we need to be constantly open to a spiritual change within ourselves. The planet does not exist just to be subservient to human needs and aspirations. My Celtic forbears, centuries ago, saw no disconnection between their Christian faith and nature. They befriended it in a straightforward way, intuitively recognizing that they were 'at one' with God's creation. This fact was underlined in their daily prayer:

> Bless to me, O God, the moon that is above me,
> Bless to me, O God, the earth that is beneath me.

They walked in harmony with the changing seasons, not in some falsely romantic way but rather because they believed that God's power permeated the winds, rain and sunshine. And that same God protected not only them, but also their animals on which they depended for survival. This prayer not only asks God to watch over their cattle but is filled with gratitude for the very pastures themselves:

> Pastures smooth, long, spreading,
> Grassy meads aneath your feet;
> The friendship of God the Son to bring you home
> To the field of the fountains.

In mentioning these prayers, I am very aware that our post-modern communities cannot be compared directly with that of rural societies which existed more than a thousand years ago. Yet from this ancient wisdom of the Celtic people we can discover certain insights which may be able to illumine our present efforts to connect humanity in a more imaginative way with the natural order. That task begins by reflecting deeply on our apparent insatiable need

to 'dominate' our environment rather than to befriend it. Can we learn again to stand humbly before the immense mystery of nature and to be able again to listen to its often muted but myriad voices; to recognize, as Dean Carter says in his poem 'Sanctuary', our essential naivety in the face of Creation's incredibly complex unfolding:

> At the door of this living cathedral
> Of rock, soil, cloud,
> Beech, oak, congregated,
> I claim sanctuary.
> I claim sanctuary
> From my own stupidity,
> From my own naivety,
> From my own rapacity.
> After blundering like a wounded animal
> Through the undergrowth of life,
> Here
> The finely sculpted clouds
> At the other side of sunset
> Hold the light for me –
> A black crow flashes a white underwing
> In welcome.

Dean Carter[2]

Can we imagine ourselves to be standing each day at the door of a living cathedral? Can we be a friend of the earth, perhaps in ways which we never ever dreamed as being possible? Can we express penitence about the way in which we have blundered like a wounded animal over the flowing streams and olive trees mentioned in the book of Deuteronomy? Can we again, as this Native American prayer invites us, walk quietly on the beautiful trail?

Now Talking God
With your feet I walk;
I walk with your limbs,
I carry forth your body.
For me your mind thinks,
Your voice speaks for me.
Beauty is before me,
And beauty is behind me.
Above and below me hovers the beautiful;
I am surrounded by it,
I am immersed in it,
In my youth I am aware of it,
And in old age I shall walk quietly
The beautiful trail.

Native American Prayer[3]

5

Listening to the post-modern world

Our contemporary theological task can win itself a new credibility and social relevance only through an intellectually responsible account of Christian faith which meets the demands both of the gospel and of the third millennium. We need this account for the journey into a period of world history that has been characterised as post-modern.

Hans Kung[1]

Dear Tom,

Thanks for your letter. You tell me bluntly that you have no idea what the term 'post-modern' means, and you demand an explanation of it! That's a tall order, as there are about a thousand definitions of this word floating around. However, I'll try, seeing you're such a good friend!

Social thinkers regard the 'modern' period as beginning with the 18th-century Enlightenment which saw what was called 'the triumph of reason'. From this womb sprang the massive achievements of science and technology, and much of the western world began to be described as 'secular' – liberated from a world-view based on religious experience. This rational world-view dominated the 20th century. It carried within it many assumptions – that western culture was 'superior'; that under-developed nations would eventually become 'developed' – i.e. like Europe or the States; that faith in God was a purely personal matter; that science would answer all our questions and that the natural world existed solely for the use and abuse of humankind. This is only a brief summary.

This modern world gave birth to enormous benefits for the whole human family, but in the later years of the 20th century, people began to see that some of its underlying assumptions were flawed. The world was not monolithic, but plural; voices on the margins were not to be silenced but listened to; science was not able to provide all the solutions; 'development' was not just about whole nations taking on board western culture; the earth was precious and yet it was being polluted and destroyed in the name of 'progress'. And from these new perceptions arose what we call the 'post-modern' period.

This post-modern time is seen as very threatening by many people – because in it the old certainties have disappeared. One marker of it is that everything – literally every-thing – can be questioned. There is no such thing as 'absolute truth' because all thinking is humanly constructed – deter-mined by cultural practices. The great moral and ethical questions facing humankind all become relative, and even our individual identities are constantly open to change. In such a climate, relationships become easily disposable and cynicism becomes the prevailing mood.

If all that sounds a bit gloomy, it is! There are many dimensions within post-modernity which, for myself at least, are distinctly unattractive. A totally depressing view of it was given by one commentator: 'The prevailing temper is a wry, seen-it-all-before detachment, and etiquette demands that all judgements are delivered with an ironic half-smile.' The same person also went on to say that we have not only stopped believing in God but we have stopped believing in ourselves.

Having said that, I also recognize that our post-modern world has also a creative, gentler side, and that it has birthed huge amounts of wisdom, compassion, acceptance and spirituality. It's a paradox. One thing is certain: our present age holds together many contradictory strands. To take an example. All over the western world, institutional religion is on the decrease while at the same time the number of people seeking a spiritual dimension in their lives has shot up.

For those who are trying to follow Christ, it often appears that much in this post-modern period is opposed to the gospel; that it undermines biblical truth. But is that the case? Is it not also true that this is a moment of tremendous opportunity for the Christian churches? For them to discover new and imaginative ways of communicating the message of Jesus? Is it not, as many are now saying, a time for the churches to be prophetic, to walk in new ways of solidarity with those on the margins, to be in dialogue with those who seek an authentic spirituality and to celebrate the many streams of compassion which are evident in our society?

Post-modern ideas have left their trace in every cultural discipline from architecture to zoology, taking in on the way biology, forestry, geography, history, law, literature, the arts, medicine, politics, philosophy, sexuality: the list is endless. Whether we like it or not, we are all citizens in a world permeated by post-modern beliefs and practices. That is exciting, even if overwhelming.

In a range of different ways, our times are also uncertain and uprooting. The philosopher Ulrich Beck talks about 'risk-societies' which are characterized by waves of current surging through them; convulsing communities in rapid social shifts. He points to the enormous changes taking place in our techno-economic systems, to the intensification of social inequalities, to the destruction of nature and to the continuing transformation of work and employment models. All of these movements give birth to new types of risk; a factor in all contemporary communities is that many issues are unpredictable.

Yet my own belief is that in the midst of these massive changes we have not rejected a belief in God. Recent statistics show that around 70 per cent of British people believe in God, although the majority would not be in touch with institutional religion. Our age has not thrown overboard 'a sense of the sacred' although it has, by and large, turned away from a cultural Christianity which placed God at the apex of a hierarchical social order. It is also widely recognized, although some church members find it hard to accept, that there are innumerable ways in which to express the Christian faith – a fact which in no way undermines the teaching of Jesus! We can find God in a rock concert as well as in a Sunday morning service.

The more I read the Bible, I am faced with a God who seems to be constantly shattering all established orders and breaking new ground. The Old and New Testaments provide us with a picture of a God who welcomes, liberates, renews and heals pilgrim people. This is a God not confined to temples or churches, but One who transforms the earth, disturbs the comfortable, refuses to settle down in any one culture and who every day calls forth our creative energy. And propelled by such a God, the church on earth is always ready to encounter radical change and risk. In such times as ours, its voice must be one of hope, not of fear, as it moves with the times, not forgetting its first obedience to the living God.

Listening to the post-modern world

In writing to you in this way, Tom, I know you will respond with your own views. That will be great, as we need to keep asking the questions about modern society. It is sometimes a scary exercise, but also an exciting one. It is certainly a task which the churches must undertake in the years ahead.

Not long ago, I read something by the writer Brendan Walsh who believes, as I do, that we see hopeful signs in our post-modern society, even as we acknowledge its flaws, failures and huge uncertainties. I want to close by quoting some of his words which help me to place my own questions and doubts about some current trends in a wider framework:

> There are arguments to be had about the underlying values and quality of contemporary culture but no-one, surely, can fail to recognise that it is immensely varied and complicated. Beside the hopelessness and despair there is moral seriousness, a desire to find the good life in a confusing and brutal world. It is in many ways a more thoughtful, kinder culture, more concerned about injustice and discrimination than any before it. Traditional theology and philosophy may have run out of steam but people are discovering the sacred in new and unexpected spaces, in work for social justice, in new kinds of commitment and public ritual. Alongside the dreary repetition, the dross and kitsch of contemporary culture, there is plenty of surprise and invention. Fusions and cross-fertilisations of different ethnic traditions and especially the impact of new communications technologies have stirred up the cultural gene pool. It is interesting out there. Intelligent listening, sifting and discernment would be welcome.
>
> *Brendan Walsh*[2]

And just before I finally sign off! As I was sending this note to you, a friend who is a parish minister rang with a question. Guess what it was! Liz asked: 'Can you come over sometime and share some of your views about modern society with my congregation.' I think I'll just send her a copy of this letter!

With warm wishes. We will always be pilgrims and seekers, and the road ahead is full of bends,

Peter

6

Reconnecting with our depths

I ask God from the wealth of his glory
to give you power
through his Spirit
to be strong in your inner selves,
and I pray that Christ will make his home
in your hearts through faith.

I pray that you may have
your roots and foundations
in love,
so that you,
together with all God's people,
may have the power to understand
how broad and long,
how high and deep,
is Christ's love.

Yes, may you come to know his love,
although it can never be fully known,
and be filled with
the very nature of God.

Ephesians 3:14–21

Perhaps the greatest danger to our humanity within today's culture lies in being disconnected from our depths. Within each person is a whole cluster of capacities of the heart – for wonder, searching, listening, receptivity and life options for compassion and love. Only through experiences that reach and liberate the imagination and the heart can we discover the deepest languages of our humanity.

Paul Gallagher, writer and priest[1]

Believing is the hard bit. When others talk of their faith – whatever they believe – they seem to me to hold it with a fixedness which eludes me. What I believe falters and fluctuates week by week, day by day. Sometimes I am seized with a conviction of Christ as a person whose presence I feel; at other times my sense of the divine is merely some abstract sum of all the goodness, virtue and aspiration of humanity through all ages. Yet there is always enough. I blunder along, stumbling between community and withdrawal, oscillating between involvement and reflection, between acting on the obvious and attempting to catch glimpses of the mystical. Through it all nags the conviction that God has more to say to me, and something for me to do.

Paul Vallely, journalist and worker for justice[2]

In learning from the great faith traditions of the world, our own understanding of God is enlarged, not diminished. Buddhism reminds us of the practice of 'mindfulness': to know in each moment what is going on within and all around us.

When the Buddha was asked, 'Sir, what do your monks

practice?', he replied, 'We sit, we walk and we eat.' The questioner continued, 'But sir, everyone sits, walks and eats', and the Buddha told him 'When we sit, we *know* we are sitting. When we walk, we *know* we are walking. When we eat, we *know* we are eating.' Most of the time, we are lost in the past or carried away by future projects and concerns. When we are mindful, touching deeply into the present moment, we can see and listen at new inner depths; we enter into a new awareness of the potential inherent in each particle of time.

Thich Nhat Hanh, a Vietnamese Zen master, poet and peace activist, has been a Buddhist monk for over 40 years. Today he lives at Plum Village, a meditation community in south western France, where he teaches, writes, gardens and aids refugees world-wide. Martin Luther King, shortly before his assassination, wrote about him in memorable words : 'I do not personally know of anyone more worthy of the Nobel Peace Prize than this gentle Buddhist monk, who I am privileged to call my friend. He is a holy man, for he is humble and devout. He is a scholar of immense intellectual capacity. His ideas for peace, if applied, would build a monument to world brotherhood, to humanity.'

In one of his books, Thich Nhat Hanh compares this practice of mindfulness with the Holy Spirit. He sees both as agents of healing. When an individual has mindfulness, the capacities for love and understanding become deeper and the wounds of the soul are healed. Through mindfulness, we touch into those seeds of healing which are present in every person. As a young Buddhist novice monk, one of the first practices he learned was to breathe in and out consciously, to touch each breath with mindfulness, bringing the mind and body into alignment. Bringing stillness to his restless heart through reflecting on simple words:

Breathing in, I calm my body.
Breathing out, I smile.
Dwelling in the present moment,
I know this is a wonderful moment.

Thich Nhat Hanh[3]

As I try to understand, albeit in a fragmentary way, something of Christ's teaching, I recognize that much is said in
the Gospels about living creatively in the present moment;
God's moment which carries at its heart the invitation to be
fully alive. And such awareness of the present moment is
not possible without mindfulness; without an inner stillness which is in itself the fruit of confronting our lack of
harmony.

Observing and learning to handle our body, breathing,
feelings, mental states and consciousness is not going to
happen overnight! The practice of mindfulness does not
just fall off the wall, but even to be still for a few moments
can be the start of an extraordinary journey into a deeper
awareness of God's intentions for our lives.

One aspect of the New Testament stories which I have
always been attracted to is the fact that Jesus seemed to
have time for everyone he met. He was present to those he
encountered on the dusty roads of Palestine not just with
his body, but with his eyes, his heart and his limitless
compassion. And in that mindful awareness, he drew out
the goodness, holiness and creativity of the other person.
We can call it a 'healing touch' or an 'outreaching in love'
but whatever description is given of Christ's encounters,
their depth of meaning sprang from what our Buddhist
friends would call 'the practice of mindfulness'.

Thich Nhat Hanh's insights disclose much that can
widen our horizons as we read about the multi-faceted

ministry of Jesus. In a society obsessed with rushing around from morning until nightfall, his life-empowering words allow us to revisit what we call in India 'the cave of the heart'.

> Our true home is in the present moment. The miracle is not to walk on water. The miracle is to walk on the green earth in the present moment. Peace is all around us – in the world and in nature – and within us in our bodies and in our spirits. Once we learn to touch this peace, we will be healed and transformed. It is a matter of practice. We need only to bring our body and mind into the present moment, and we will touch what is refreshing, healing and wondrous.[4]

Active mindfulness: that awareness of the present moment which is woven into a gloriously evocative prayer which my Celtic forbears handed down through the generations:

> Thanks to Thee, O God, that I have risen today,
> To the rising of this life itself;
> May it be to Thine own glory, O God of every gift,
> And to the glory of my soul likewise.
>
> O great God, aid Thou my soul
> With the abiding of thine own mercy;
> Even as I clothe my body with wool,
> Cover Thou my soul with the shadow of Thy wing.
>
> Help me to avoid every sin,
> And the source of every sin to forsake;
> And as the mist scatters on the crest of the hills,
> May each ill haze clear from my soul, O God.

Gaelic Traditional

Discerning what really matters: being able to hear God's voice through the cacophony of other sounds which fill our waking hours – and sometimes our sleeping ones! Long ago, the psalmist struggled with the same things as we do, yet also yearned to connect with his depths – to be in touch with that whole cluster of capacities in his heart for wonder, receptivity and love.

> Teach me, LORD, the meaning of your laws, and I will
>   obey them at all times.
> Explain your law to me, and I will obey it; I will keep it
>   with all my heart.
> Keep me obedient to your commandments, because in
>   them I find happiness.
> Give me the desire to obey your laws rather than to get
>   rich.
> Keep me from paying attention to what is worthless;
>   be good to me as you have promised.
> Keep your promise to me, your servant –
>   the promise you make to those who obey you.
> I want to obey your commands;
>   give me new life, for you are righteous.

Psalm 119:33–38, 40

7

Praying

One of my favourite hymns has in it this verse:

> There've been times when I've turned from his presence
> and I've walked other paths, other ways.
> But I've called on his name
> in the dark of my shame,
> and his mercy was gentle as silence.[1]

The famous theologian, Karl Barth, said that in our praying God is really inviting us to live with him. That view of prayer is expressed in these lines. The individual is recognizing the need for God's guidance and presence, and calls out, in faith, that their life will be brought back onto a clearer path. And as they seek God's mercy, that 'still small voice' announces itself, and divine assurance enfolds them. The prayer may have been only a couple of words, or a waiting in silence: what matters is that inner journey of 'returning home' to the One who is always holding open the door of life and truth.

Yet often we see 'prayer' – in whatever form it takes – as something that *we* do. We keep wondering if we have 'got it right' – in terms of our thoughts and faltering words. And because we often reach the conclusion that we don't 'have it right', we give up on praying altogether. And there is another piece to this. Some people believe that prayer should be left to the clerics – after all, it's their job! Yet if prayer does not belong right at the heart of ordinary, daily living, where does it belong?

For centuries, women and men who have made prayer their total way of life, have reminded us that God first comes to us – long before there is even the slightest thought of praying in our own minds. One person who encouraged many others to experience the power of prayer in their lives was Julian of Norwich. She wrote these memorable words: 'Never forget that we have all been loved by God from before the very beginning.' That's amazing, and it puts our anxieties about what we should think and say in our prayers into perspective. God is there before us, and, as St Paul says, even when we have no idea what to say, the Spirit prays on our behalf.

In recent years, Helder Camara, a Roman Catholic bishop in Brazil, has become a truly inspirational figure for many of us around the world. He died in the summer of 1999, but his work of love and solidarity on behalf of the exploited will long be remembered. I find his prayers to be both challenging and reassuring at the same time. He once wrote to the people in his diocese some words on prayer at a time when they were enduring horrific suffering. He talks of 'putting our ear to the ground' in order to hear the Lord's voice: to recognize that God always is by our side, even when in our agony we are silenced and unable to think at all.

> Put your ear to the ground
> and listen,
> hurried, worried footsteps,
> bitterness, rebellion.

Praying

Hope
hasn't yet begun.
Listen again.
Put out your feelers.
The Lord is there.

Helder Camara[2]

Is this not the essence of prayer – to see the One who is always near, and who is constantly inviting us, in gentle compassion, to come back to our inheritance as a human being made in the divine image? That fact made it possible for St Paul to write these powerful words to the Christian believers in Rome in the first century: 'For I am certain that nothing can separate us from his love, neither the present nor the future, neither angels nor other heavenly rulers, – there is nothing in all creation that will ever be able to separate us from the love of God which is ours through Christ Jesus our Lord.' (Romans 8:38–39).

In her beautiful book, *Praying our Goodbyes*, Joyce Rupp spoke of 'God's fireflies', these countless intimations of our Creator's presence which flit in and out of our lives day by day. Like the fireflies, they come and go in an instant, sometimes almost unseen, except for a momentary flash. I warm to that comparison, because it underlines that often our prayers are spontaneous, provisional and immediate. We speak of 'arrow prayers' – these exclamations such as 'thank you, Lord' which almost unconsciously arise from our hearts in certain circumstances.

Although praying is a serious matter, when it becomes merely an intellectual heavy-duty experience, its life-giving core has been lost. Can we walk on a gentle path with our prayers? By that I mean, seeing them as a natural conversation with the God who brought us all here in the first place.

We are not conversing with a stranger, but with One who understands us so much more that we understand ourselves. From what we read in the Gospels, Jesus was much more concerned with the way in which we come to our prayers than with the words. That is abundantly clear in the parable of the Pharisee and the tax collector (Luke 18: 9–14).

If praying was all about words, we would be missing the point. Perhaps that is why I feel at home with Sheila Cassidy's valuable wisdom on the matter. Sheila has written on various dimensions of spirituality, but in these few words she brings home a basic fact about personal prayer. Her viewpoint is earthed in the conviction that God first approaches us – constantly inviting us into the listening place. As the hymn says, Christ's healing and forgiving love is 'as gentle as silence' and enters what we call in India 'the cave of the heart'.

> When people ask me what I pray for, I say I don't pray for anything: I pray because God *is*. I sit before him open like an empty bowl, like a flower, like a wound. I give him my joy, my confusion, my boredom, my pain – just lay it there on the floor for him to process how he wishes and when he is ready.
>
> *Sheila Cassidy*[3]

God is. Do we believe that not as an abstract idea, but as the base line of our whole lives? For it is this tough question which, at the end of the day, and when all the chips are down, makes sense of our prayers. In other words, makes them 'part of us': authentic expressions of what we are in our guts. This is not about precise words or faultless grammar. Far from it. It is about who we really are with all our contradictions and hesitations conversing with the One who holds the whole world in his hands.

If we look at the prayers in the book of Psalms, on page after page we see human beings like ourselves wrestling with their God. These prayers are passionate conversations between the writer and his God. Every emotion in the book is held within them – anger, jealousy, rage, laughter, agony, hope, sorrow, gratitude . . . the list is endless. All of life is here, and we see no disconnection between faith in God and ordinary living. This is no Sunday religion, but a life-giving dialogue which is up-front, energized and brutally honest. And some of it is born of that anguish with which we can identify:

> My God, my God, why have you abandoned me?
> I have cried desperately for help, but still it does not
>   come.
> During the day I call to you, my God, but you do not
>   answer;
> I call at night, but get no rest.
> But you are enthroned as the Holy One,
> the one whom Israel praises.
> Our ancestors put their trust in you;
> they trusted you and you saved them.
> They called to you and escaped from danger;
> they trusted you and were not disappointed.
>
> *Psalm 22:1–5*

Even when they were miles away doing their own thing, the people of Israel did not forget that when they put their feelers out, as Helder Camara said to his people in Brazil, the Lord would be there. Hope was real; the promises of

God were not empty ones. Nor were they empty in the comforting words of Jesus. He kept telling his rather obstinate disciples not to be discouraged, and to keep on praying however hard the road ahead. He longed for them to see God as if he were their own mother and father which is why he said to them '. . . you know how to give good things to your children. How much more, then, will the Father in heaven give the Holy Spirit to those who ask him!' (Luke 11:13).

As I see it, our praying will always remain rather empty and dry, if we forget that it is fundamentally a natural conversation between ourselves and our God. In our churches there is a place for imaginatively-constructed prayers spoken with clarity. Yet deep within me, I believe that Christ, who himself walked with much pain and mis-understanding, is just as near the heroin addict battling for his very life and screaming out through his tears: 'Lord, if you are anywhere now, help me please.'

Many of us need to revisit our understanding of prayer because we have turned a special gift of God into a formalized experience. We know only too well our own needs yet somehow we feel ashamed or afraid to bring them to God. If that is the case, then we have forgotten that hand of unlimited love which is always, and everywhere, stretched out to us.

Again and again I come back to that simple phrase 'let go and let God'. It may be very basic in its language but it contains a profound truth. Can we re-learn how to 'be present' to God? Listening, waiting, expecting – allowing God, as Sheila Cassidy says, to process all that is going on in our lives at the moment. Offering to Christ all of our selves, and not just those parts which we feel are all right to express. And such prayer, over a period, will propel us more and more into God's world in all of its plurality and surprise.

Jock Dalrymple, who was a spiritual guide to many, put it succinctly:

> Praying leads us straight into the heart of mystery where we find that words fail, concepts no longer help, knowing gives way to unknowing. At this point we feel insecure and lost; no longer in control. Yet if we do not give up and turn back, we will be rewarded with a peace that does pass understanding and the experience of being grasped by God. At that place we discover not only our true selves, but also our neighbour and God's creation in all of its goodness and glory. That is what God intends to happen to us all.
>
> *Jock Dalrymple*[4]

or in the famous words of Saint Patrick:

> Christ be beside me,
> Christ be before me,
> Christ be behind me,
> King of my heart.
> Christ be within me,
> Christ be below me,
> Christ be above me,
> Never to part.

8

Realizing God is not always a man!

Blessed is She who spoke and the world became.
  Blessed is She.
Blessed is She who in the beginning gave birth.
Blessed is She who says and performs.
Blessed is She who declares and fulfils.
Blessed is She whose womb covers the earth . . .
Blessed is She who lives forever, and exists eternally.
Blessed is She who redeems and saves. Blessed is Her
  Name.

Sabbath Prayer[1]

There may be many uncertainties in the world, but we can be sure that God need not always be spoken of as male! In trying to reach an understanding of God, we can use both male and female images and metaphors. Divine truth is fathomless and our words can never describe God fully. The writer C.S. Lewis was quite clear on this. He noted that our 'personal ideas' about God are not 'divine ideas'. The fact is that God is neither male nor female, and is always bringing us to new insights about the eternal mystery. For example, one of the Iona liturgies uses a wonderfully evocative description of God as 'the midwife of change'. I like that very much!

Realizing God is not always a man!

Afua Kuma lives and works on a small farm in the northern part of Ghanaian West Africa. She is a well-known and skilled nurse in her local community and an active member of the local church. Her prayers in the Twi language (a major language in West Africa) take us into the heart of African religious experience. As I studied them, in translation, I realized that in her naming of God, we in the West have much to learn.

The God who Afua encounters can be in farm and forest, and amid the customs and structures of African traditional life. In her vital prayers we are privileged to share a humble farmer's grasp of Christ. She uses familiar images of her environment to express the attributes to God such as omnipotence, which we usually think of in the abstract. The way in which she speaks of God is shaped by her physical world. Or to put it another way, her theology is not separate from daily life, but a feature of it. The more I read Afua's prayers, the more astonished I was at how many names she used for Christ. Here are some of them:

'The Fearless One' 'The Grinding Stone' 'The Hunter'
   'The Torrent'
'The String of God Beads' 'The River' 'The Source of
   Flowing Waters'
'The Holy One' 'The Untiring Potter' "The Great
   Forest Canopy'
'The Wind and the Storm' 'The Water-lily' 'The Tall
   Mountain'
'The Hard-working Farmer' 'The Magnificent Tree'
'The Eggs of the Green Mamba' 'The Powerful Chief'
   'The Rock'
'The Elephant Hunter' 'The Master of Signs and
   Wonders'

'The Humble King' 'The Master of Wisdom'
'Wonder worker' 'The Cornerstone'

And there are many more!

In fact, I counted up more than 180 different titles used by Afua Kuma for Jesus, all of them rooted in her personal experience as a rural African woman. Some of these titles related to 'chieftaincy' such as 'Chief among Chiefs' or 'The Big House which takes in Travellers'. Some related to nature such as the beautiful description of Christ as 'The Best of Yams'. Others spoke of Christ as a hunter or warrior such as 'The Deep Forest Hunter' or 'The One who sets your heart thumping'.

Afua also talks of Christ in ways which relate directly to the local community and to domestic life: 'The Giver of Shea-nut Oil' or 'The Day of the Month when I get my Pay' or 'The Brightest of Lanterns'. Or again in biblical imagery: 'Saviour of the Poor' or 'Master of Wisdom' or 'Guide to the Blind'. Aware of my own limited abilities to describe God, Afua opens up new paths in prayer and in the way I visualize God. For her, God is a dynamic force – the One who creates, regulates and harmonizes all the powers in the universe, animate and inanimate. Weaving through all her amazing prayers is a sense of awe, of reverence and of mystery. She stands before her God as a humble supplicant, recognizing that 'the way we live' and 'the way we believe' are different sides of the one coin. For example: 'If you meet other evil persons, do not fear. Jesus is a cutlass going before you.' (Could St Paul have phrased it better?)

In this lyrical prayer, Afua, in describing Christ in a variety of ways, also shows us how to make our description of God meaningful in a local context. In a western urban situation we would not employ the same metaphors as

Afua does, but she is a guide showing us routes into truly imaginative prayer and praise.

> The great Rock, we hide behind you:
> You are the Great Forest Canopy, giving cool shade:
> The Big Tree which lifts its vines
> to peep at heaven.
> You are the Magnificent Tree whose dripping leaves
> encourage the luxuriant growth below;
> You weave the streams like plaited hair,
> and with fountains you tie a knot.

It is crucial that we comprehend the reality of God as always being beyond our frail words and definitions. We too easily tie God down, and in doing so discourage many of those who are genuine seekers, despite their doubts and hesitations. Our church language can be totally off-putting; a barrier to belief. Yet most of us long for images of God, and words about God, which touch into our emotions and carry us into new depths of faith. We are all comfortable with different ways of expressing truth and if calling God 'Mother' is not helpful, that's OK – as long as we remember that it may be tremendously meaningful for others.

I leave the last thought with Afua Kuma. She sees Christ both as Diviner and Builder – understanding the secrets of all hearts. The water diviner pinpoints the hidden wells, deep in the earth. Christ sees us not as we appear to be, but as we truly are. A truth held in this prayer where Christ is portrayed as 'Builder of the House' – and a woman builder at that!

She is the Builder of the House.
She builds with work and care,
and behold, it turns to a house of glass!
the Builder sees the hearts of all inside,
no matter where they stand.

9

Rediscovering community

Eat and drink together,
talk and laugh together,
enjoy life together;
but never call it friendship
until we have wept together.

Traditional African saying

This world needs one ethic. Our society does not need a uniform religion or a uniform ideology but it does need binding norms, values, ideals and goals.

Hans Küng[1]

Many miracles and wonders were being done through the apostles, and everyone was filled with awe. All the believers continued together in close fellowship and shared their belongings with one another.

Acts 2:43–44

I sought for my soul, but my soul failed to see:
I sought my God, but my God eluded me:
I sought my brother, and found all three!

Inscribed on a wall at Anandwan Ashram in India
where many people with leprosy have found a home

India faces multiple problems, but it has also much to teach us. Even in the face of rapid urbanization, its many faces still reveal a way of community living which has been lost in our society. That is not to suggest that we can transplant an Indian model to our own shores, but living in that great land illumined for me how this sense of belonging and being accountable to one another has disappeared from our midst.

The last hundred years, in western communities, has seen the individual becoming lonelier and more isolated from others. Friends in Africa and India are amazed when they learn that in our country, folk can die in their homes and not be found for several weeks. Dead behind their own front door, but without anyone knowing. They find it impossible to believe that not one single other person would call at their house over the course of a few weeks. And they contrast that kind of isolation with the endless comings and goings in their own homes. It is still true that in many parts of the world it takes a whole village to raise a child.

Having said this, I also believe that our western societies are now searching, at a whole variety of levels, for the restoration of 'community' – a word often heard these days from Government officials. It has become a buzz word; a warm word: community policing, community care, community studies, youth and community work, community churches. George Hillery listed ninety-four uses of the term, the only feature they had in common being a concern about people. Despite this wide usage, the basic question remains: can 'community' in the sense of people being mutually accountable to one another ever return in a society which prizes so highly the individual and personal self-enhancement?

During my years of working at Iona Abbey, I met
hundreds of people, from around the world, who were
involved, one way or another, with the restoration of local
communities. Bridge-builders, who were often working in
areas where there had been a total breakdown of the
common life, or where different cultural and religious
traditions encountered one another only in conflict and
misunderstanding. These folk are trail-blazers for the rest
of us, as we search for new forms of communal identity
and purpose. Brother Roget of Taizé speaks of genuine
community being radiant and making visible Christ's own
face. The bridge-builders are often radiant people themselves, seeing beyond all these artificial barriers which
imprison us, even in our affluence and mobility.

Yet in this search for 'community' in our modern world,
which is marked by its plurality, it is not possible to retreat
to some notion of the common life rooted in an idealized
model of rural living. If the churches of the West are to be
prophetically engaged with the rebuilding of our common
life, then this task must be primarily grounded in the
vibrancy and fragmentation of the metropolis; in the din
of the city. It begins with a compassionate awareness of
contemporary cultures which at first glance may appear
completely 'secular'. Listening to these plural cultures and
walking with them, not in some harsh crusading spirit but
in order to be an instrument of genuine reconciliation
amidst both believers and non-believers.

Rediscovering authentic community within our present
fragmentations is essentially 'a work of love', as these
bridge-builders have shown. Reaching out, accepting the
fact that Christ's peace may take us into uncomfortable
places. In the First Letter of John we read: 'God is love and
whoever lives in love lives in union with God and God lives

with them: love is made perfect in us.' Within these beautiful words is held the primary energy and underlying wisdom of community. Or to put it another way: can we reach out to 'the stranger' without a recognition that Christ is continually reaching out to us in forgiving love?

Rediscovering out essential community with one another is a long-haul task. Much in present society militates against it. Perhaps we can be strengthened in our search for a more life-giving common life when we recognize the face of Jesus in the other person. Such a perception of 'the other' propels us out of our self-absorbed life-styles. It underlines the fact, as the gospel reminds us, that we are not really in a position to understand even a fragment of the mystery of Christ's love, if we have not first walked in companionship with our sisters and brothers. Looking at the global situation, we see glimpses of this deep-rooted solidarity present in re-energized communities. The Celtic Christian recognized that Christ is always present in the stranger's guise – a truth expressed in the rune of hospitality:

> We saw a stranger yesterday,
> We put food in the eating place,
> Drink in the drinking place,
> Music in the listening place,
> And, with the sacred name of the triune God,
> He blessed us and our house,
> Our cattle and our dear ones.
> As the lark says in her song:
> Often, often, often,
> Goes Christ in the stranger's guise.

Around us many familiar landmarks have either disappeared or are vanishing. It is, for many, a threatening time and a time of great risk. Even within affluent nations, we feel insecure and uncertain about the future. In such a situation we desperately need one another! Isolation leads to all types of disintegration, and we can take small first steps towards community by opening ourselves up to the issues within our local communities. Trusting the other; allowing ourselves, perhaps for the first time, to be vulnerable to 'the stranger' who is actually our sister or brother.

One sign of hope lies in the fact that we are awakening to our basic interdependence; our connectedness. Millions of us share many of the same questions, fears and insecurities. They are spiritual questions for they are about our shared humanity. They are also about the acceptance and understanding of difference. Whatever the future holds, we will be a multi-cultural society in which many differing traditional cultural threads will meet and interact.

It is not particularly fashionable to speak of mutual accountability, but the message of the Bible constantly draws us back to this truth. We see it clearly in the history of the Jewish people – accountability to God and to one another. In the New Testament, this truth is a central thread in the teaching of Christ. In the Sermon on the Mount, Jesus says that to be his follower or disciple carries within it the challenge to be 'a light' for our communities. This is not an injunction to keep ourselves to ourselves, but rather a powerfully expressed invitation to be right there in the midst of society, in all of its contradictions and uncertainties, as a people radiating God's presence. Quite a thought!

You are like a light for the whole world. A city built on a hill cannot be hidden. No one lights a lamp and puts it under a bowl; instead a person puts it on a lampstand where it gives light to everyone in the house. In the same way, your light must shine before people, so that they will see the good things you do and praise your Father in heaven.

Matthew 5:14–16

If local churches can forget their internal problems and move away from being interested only in mere survival, they become, under the guidance of the Holy Spirit, these living 'signs of community' for others. In the ecumenical Taizé Community, they speak of the local churches as being 'parables of community', places of outreach which, in Vaclav Havel's phrase, 'live in truth'. And this very notion of 'living in truth' means that a local congregation is inescapably open to the surrounding community and sensitive to its needs. These congregations become the opposite of religious ghettos as they recognize that 'living in truth' is not only going to be a costly form of obedience to the gospel, but that it will open alternative ways of 'being church', counter-cultural expressions of church, in which hope at its deepest level can be nourished.

It is the working of the Holy Spirit which can enable local congregations to discern how these truths are lived out meaningfully in a local context. 'Living in truth' may lead a small congregation to stand in solidarity with those who have lost their jobs through a local factory closure, or it may involve its members being part of a group to campaign for debt relief at a global level. In such activity, locally-based Christians embody a working model of community, which carries no hidden agendas and looks for no pay-back; an authentic 'sign of community' for our times.

Therefore in this long search to rediscover a sense of community which is appropriate in our age, the Christian churches when they are spiritually alive and prayerfully aware of the society around them, can offer hope. Even with their reduced numbers, congregations can be powerful parables of community when they begin to reach out and leave behind their own anxieties. In listening to the multiple voices within society, the churches can discover new depths of spirituality within themselves as they seek to express what many have termed 'a radical Christian witness' free from vague platitudes and simplistic phrases about God. That understanding of Christian witness which works towards both the recovery of authentic community and social holiness.

People come and go in the market place;
they see others in different hues;
here there are black and white, indigenous and immigrant,
a rainbow people but truly together,
a people of one family.
We seek to bear each other's burdens;
we seek to share each other's joys;
we share our happiness and our sorrows;
why then do some make us enemies?
We are one family, God's people,
a rainbow people whose song is love.

Geoffrey Duncan[2]

10

Tagore's light

Our first task in approaching another people, another culture, another religion, is to take off our shoes for the place we are approaching is holy and we may find ourselves treading on another's dream. More serious still, we may forget that God was there before our arrival.

Shared in a cross-cultural workshop

The great Indian writer, philosopher and poet, Rabindranath Tagore has been a strong influence on my life. He died in 1941, six years before independence came to India, but he is still regarded as one of the founding fathers of the nation. The ashram which he founded was called Shanti Niketan and it became, not only a centre of learning, but also a significant national symbol in the non-violent movements, led by Gandhi, which eventually brought independence from Britain.

From Shanti Niketan
in a less frenetic age,
Tagore
who gave so much
of India's spirit

to the world,
penned words
illumining
our human journey.

Gentle words, but deep:
thoughts that would
speak to the heart,
enlarging its capacity to care.

Could we not,
amidst our endless business,
listen to them again?

Could we not,
amidst our uncertainties,
let them penetrate our soul
and bring healing?

Could we not,
amidst
all the divisions
and pain of our times,
allow them to remind us
of
another Reality?

Gentle words, but deep,
speaking with clarity
through the contradictions of our times . . .

   'Lord,
   send me your love,
   that keeps my heart still
   with the fullness of peace.'

11

Sharing our stories

God created a reminder, an image.
Humanity is a reminder of God:
as God is compassionate,
let humanity be compassionate.
Abraham Heschel[1]

Blessed be the works of your hands, O Holy One.
Blessed be these hands that have touched life.
Blessed be these hands that have nurtured creativity.
Blessed be these hands that have held pain.
Blessed be these hands that have embraced with passion.
Blessed be these hands that have tended gardens.
Blessed be these hands that have closed in anger.
Blessed be these hands that have planted new seeds.
Blessed be these hands that have harvested ripe fields.
Blessed be these hands that have cleaned, washed,
    mopped, scrubbed.
Blessed be these hands that have become knotty with age.
Blessed be these hands that are wrinkled and scarred
    from doing justice.
Blessed be these hands that have reached out and been
    received.
Blessed be these hands that hold the promise of the future.
Blessed be the works of your hands, O Holy One.
Diann Neu[2]

Sharing our stories

I am a woman
and my blood
cries out.
We are millions
and strong together.
You better hear us
or you may be doomed.

Gabrielle Dietrich, theologian,
companion of the marginalized

Rigobertu Menchu, the Nobel Peace Prize winner, once made this observation: 'What hurts our rural Guatemalan people most is that our costumes are considered beautiful but it's as if the person wearing it didn't exist.' The amazingly rich life stories of these Guatemalan villagers had not been heard; what mattered to the visitor was the brilliance and variety of their clothes.

It is not only the rural families in far-off Guatemala who feel that their personal stories are of little consequence. Many people in highly technological societies, such as our own, feel the same way. 'Who is interested in what I've done with my life?' is a common refrain. And do I even have a story to tell? We all have these powerful tapes in our heads telling us that we have really not done anything special with our lives. We have nothing to report: we are 'ordinary'. In the end of the day, there is basically nothing to say. It's almost as if we did not exist.

Contemporary culture, despite the myriad forms of counselling which are available, also plays down the telling of our personal stories. We are spectators, watching every movement in the unfolding dramas held within the lives of the famous and the totally corrupt. They sure have stories: we don't. Millions make these stories their own stories, forgetting that in themselves is carried an amazing history of love and loss, laughter and agony.

Connie was a home-maker who lived on a small farm in a rather remote glen in Angus in Scotland. When we worked in South India her congregation was linked with us, and Connie, on their behalf, wrote to us regularly. In these letters she kept saying what wonderful work we were doing in India, but said practically nothing about herself or her family. One day I sent her a note saying that we were not doing particularly special things in India and that we would love to know a little about her own situation.

Almost by return of post (if such a thing is possible given the vagaries of the international postal system) Connie replied – pouring out her story, page upon page. In that letter she described a life which was filled with triumph and tragedy in equal amounts. Every line revealed glimpses of grief, courage, prayerful awareness, doubt, integrity and of a love which kept shining against all the odds. This was no tale of an idyllic life in a beautiful Angus glen, although it was punctuated by laughter and hope. It was a story of hardship and heartbreak, but also of glory in the grey.

The sharing of our stories, of our 'ordinary' stories which are in fact 'extraordinary', is something which we are slowly recovering in our churches. God longs for these stories to be told, retold and celebrated; to be laughed over and wept over; to be accepted, honoured and woven into the wider tapestry of our shared humanity. They are sacred stories, revealing in their diversity these grace-filled moments which reveal God's continuing purpose amidst humankind. In their telling we are offered the possibility of healing; of recognizing our essential rootedness both in community and in history.

Connie was brought up to believe that her personal story

was of little consequence, and was something she kept to herself. She moved through life with the assumption that God's glory was not revealed in 'the ordinary'. Yet the truth was exactly opposite. Her letter to us, in its quiet, undramatic way, revealed a life which was inspirational, faith-filled, risk-taking and life-giving. Joanna Macy, who is a peace activist in the States, says that in the sharing of our joys and griefs we discover our connections to one another. That is an undeniable fact. What is also true is that as we speak of our own pilgrimage, we connect with our story-telling God.

In his meetings with people, Jesus saw beyond their outward presentation, touching into their inner lives. He listened, and responded to their deepest longings. Inextricably intertwined with the sharing of our own stories is the whole issue of vulnerability. Many of us remain closed to our brokenness, carefully disguising and cleverly sealing off the wounds and blows life has given us. Yet it is precisely where we have suffered and known pain that we can be instruments of nourishment and hope to others – a truth we see at work in the meetings of Alcoholics Anonymous.

It only takes a few personal stories to open the floodgates of joy and anguish in others, for we all yearn to redeem the scars and amputations which mark our lives. Even in our most abandoned moments we sometimes are overwhelmed with a desire to experience anew God's lively and inviting love; to get a whiff of our own transformation, our own wholeness; to be nourished by the openness of another person, and perhaps especially by those who are our hidden neighbours, fearful of ever uttering a word lest that utterance calls down on their lives even greater marginalization.

My own question would be, can we recreate authentic community spirit without such sharing of our stories? In our privatized society, we yearn to connect and to be affirmed. Loneliness has become a central marker of our times, and not only in cities. As we journey into reconnecting with our neighbours, in the sharing of our stories, many of those who have gone through various 'hells' in their own lives can show us a way forward. Those who have been imprisoned in the world of drugs and alcohol realize what it means to share with another person the absolute agony of it all. And to tell their story not in high-flown words, but with gut-wrenching clarity. Stories from the heart with which we cannot but be connected.

Many times I have been drawn back to some words of Joyce Gunn Cairns, an artist and a member of the Iona Community. At one time Joyce worked as a volunteer in a local prison, and from her experiences there was able to put in a beautiful way something of that transformation which God gives to us as we share our own story and listen to those of others.

> The people in prison whom I visit have honoured me with their stories and with the gift of their vulnerability. Many of them are able to discern the true freedom that comes when one is stripped of all status, and it is thus that they can teach me something about the meaning of spiritual poverty. The more I listen and the more I share, I recognise not only connection, but a basic truth: in coming to serve the poor, so to speak, I discover that I am poor.

A few years ago, I lived for several months in a tiny apartment on a crowded street in South Chicago. A multicultural street. A street on which there was activity round the clock, every day of the year. I loved that street with its many faces and multiple dimensions. Yet, there was also much loneliness on that street. Separate lives passing on the pavements but not, for the most part, interacting on a personal level. And one cold night in December, late in the evening, as I sat in my own small place, surrounded by people most of whom were total strangers, I wrote this poem which could be a poem about any street in a great city. Maybe it is your street, even if it's thousands of miles from South Chicago.

Who are you, my neighbour,
on this crowded street?
We live close-by
in our tiny apartments
and share the changing seasons.
But do we know each other
not as strangers, but as friends?
Your family is far away, like mine;
yours in El Salvador, mine in Scotland –
two different worlds.
You came as refugee, I through choice;
and now we are on the same street
alone, in our tiny apartments
separated only by a wall.
And around us a vast city
glittering, yet vulnerable,
where so many like us
have found food and shelter
but not always freedom from fear.
Let's meet and talk one day
and share our stories,
and maybe our tears.

For the lights on our streets
are Christmas lights –
reminding us of another Story
where strangers meet
and find each other.
It's the story of Jesus,
the One who is always here
on East 53rd Street
in south Chicago.

I 2

Helen's wisdom

Every new birth in the world is a sign that God is not yet discouraged of humankind.

Rabindranath Tagore, Indian poet and scholar

Though I am different from you, we were born involved with one another.
T'ao Chien, poet

Helen has Down's Syndrome. We have been good friends for many years, and I recently had this letter from her father, Bill, who is a Methodist minister.

Dear Peter,

You will remember well my sharing with you the time of Helen's birth, now more than 20 years ago. Both the joy of being our first child and then for me (and in a different way for Olive) the devastation of learning that she had Down's Syndrome. It was only gradually that I moved into this new life that Helen had brought us.

This journey has had its great days, and also its rough ones. Generally speaking, it has taken us to places of much love and understanding, and acceptance. We have received support from friends and strangers, in the Down's Syndrome Association, the Christian community and from travellers sharing the same road. It has led me to find the work of Jean Vanier in the L'Arche communities, and to see disability from a new perspective. We have also found strength in the work of the Baptist Union Initiative for people with a learning disability. Helen's life has also brought me to be part of a chaplaincy team in a long-stay hospital, being with those with learning disabilities.

The years have gone on, and I am a very different person because of Helen's situation. She is now a young adult and has gone to live in a MENCAP Home-start Supported Living Project. Helen shares a house with another young adult, and the expectation is that they will, with appropriate levels of support, manage their own lives. She is a very committed member of her local Methodist church, and often comes with me to the small village churches which are part of my circuit.

Recently, when we were in a discussion group in one of these small congregations, Helen reminded us of her own journey into membership, and of the ways that people had welcomed and affirmed her life. At one point we were talking about the church in relation to the local community. Helen made a point strongly. She said that people liked to come to church for special occasions, like Harvest and Christmas and weddings, and that we should be glad about that and not bemoan the fact that they were not there at other times. Helen felt that as far as God was concerned it was OK for families to come to church when they felt comfortable with that – even if only occasionally. I was grateful for her insight. Helen has given our family so many insights. Her wisdom is very special!

Here then is another part of Helen's on-going story: it's good news.

Yours in love,

Bill

Helen's wisdom

In the Gospels, we read that Jesus saw the crowds and went up a hill, where he sat down. His disciples, still rather bewildered by all that was happening, gathered round him, and he began to teach them:

Happy are those who know they are spiritually poor;
the Kingdom of heaven belongs to them!

Happy are those who mourn;
God will comfort them!

Happy are those who are humble;
they will receive what God has promised!

Happy are those whose greatest desire is to do what God requires;
God will satisfy them fully!

Happy are those who are merciful to others;
God will be merciful to them!

Happy are those who are pure in heart;
they will see God!

Matthew 5:3–8

13

Basil and Mary's holiness

If your eye is pure,
there will be sunshine in your soul.

Matthew 6:22

Only those who themselves have been resurrected
can actually celebrate Easter.

Dorothee Soelle

Only one day before he himself passed into death, the
ninety-six year old Zen Buddhist sage, D. T. Suzuki,
wrote that we should 'aspire so to live that we, along
with Meister Eckhart, can say that "Christ is born
every minute in my soul".'

Donald Nicholl, scholar and writer

Following the death of Cardinal Basil Hume in June of
1999, hundreds of letters arrived at his former home in
Westminster. One of these came from Patrick Maguire,
one of the 'Maguire Seven' who were cleared of supplying
explosives for the Guildford pub bombings in 1974.

My family and myself were all arrested in 1974. I was
13 at the time. After the trial at the Old Bailey which

lasted for more than seven weeks, we were all sent to
prison for many years. As a boy I had always gone to
church, and I did so even when I was in prison. But I
would always ask why God had let this happen to us;
where was he when I needed him? I felt let down by my
faith and everything to do with it. So I gave up. Some
years after I was released I got a phone call from the
Archbishop's House, telling me that Cardinal Hume
would like to see me. At no time did I feel nervous or
worried about meeting this man. I knew that he had
played a very big part in helping to prove our innocence.
He had put his name at the top of our fight for justice,
and many names had followed. What a man to have on
your side! But my faith had gone. As he stood up from
the chair he had been sitting in, the room lit up as if a
thousand lights had been turned on. Standing there,
looking at him, I could see and feel so much – love, goodness, holiness. He was a giant. I felt so small. With open
arms he welcomed me to his home. We had some tea,
and talked – well, I did the talking while he listened. He
winced as I relived my story, sharing the pain with me.
After that first meeting with him, I was to see him many
more times over the years. He would have a laugh and a
joke, let his hair down, be one of the boys. I would have
loved to take him out for a beer. I bet he would have had
one! I always looked forward to seeing him. He was my
friend – who just happened to be a cardinal.

Patrick Maguire[1]

For me, that's a wonderful description of Basil Hume's life-
giving holiness. Patrick Maguire writes not of some artificial piety, but of a wholesome, healing holiness. And it is
not only the Basil Humes of this world who remind us of

this many-faceted quality. Thankfully, life-giving holiness is not limited to those who are ordained.

In the early 1970s, Dalmarnock in the East End of Glasgow bore all the hallmarks of multiple inner-city deprivation. I was parish minister there and I soon came to realize that behind the statistics about poverty were many women and men who could teach me so much about life-giving holiness. They shone. They lit up their surroundings and without ever giving it a moment's thought were 'holy folk'. And others saw that holiness in them, even if they never defined it.

Mary was a holy person. When you first met her it was her bubbling humour that struck you. It spilled over and at times ran riot. It was like a powerful shower – invigorating and free flowing, even at 7.30 in the morning! But it only took moments in her company to recognize that here, along with the humour, went warmth and a practical faith in a God who had walked with her through many dark times. She was the kind of person who could carry a whole community – and yet do it gently, always aware of her own fragility.

Often we talked together in her one-roomed home within a tenement building that was truly on its last legs. And our conversations were never just about Mary and her situation. Far from it. They were about the struggles and hopes of the community in Dalmarnock: about how we could be more active in rehousing a neighbouring family who lived in a house where even in high summer the inside walls were running with water: about how to be in solidarity with a young woman faced with increasing heroin addiction.

Mary and others in Dalmarnock reminded me of the 'Lamedvovniks' in Jewish teaching. These are thirty-six righteous people upon whom the world depends for its survival – and who also keep God's wrath off the rest of us! Their lives renew society and while Mary may never have thought that she was keeping God's judgement away from the East End of Glasgow, she was certainly lighting up her immediate neighbourhood.

The life-giving holy people run a mile from any form of adulation. Mary wanted none of that. What she did want was for her neighbours in the East End of Glasgow to keep reaching out across their different cultural and religious traditions to one another. She longed that folk would go the extra mile – and with a smile on their face as they did so.

And although she died many years before Basil Hume, they both radiated goodness and serenity of spirit in their last illnesses. On a February morning, Mary died peacefully in her own bed in that tenement building which had been home for over 40 years. Within two months it had been demolished. On the morning of her funeral, one of Mary's neighbours, a young guy who spent more time in prison than out of it, came up to me. I remember his words clearly: 'My God, she wasn't half a guid, guid wuman!'

Life-giving holiness. We recognize it, even if it is almost impossible to define. We would be a poorer society by far if we didn't have these holy folk in our neighbourhoods and in archbishops' houses. A holiness that is grounded in everyday living but which also reveals one of God's many faces. The kind of holiness expressed in a prayer which Rabindranath Tagore of India wrote many years ago:

This is my prayer to thee, my lord –
    strike, strike at the root of penury in my heart.
Give me the strength lightly to bear my joys and
    sorrows.

Give me the strength to make my love fruitful in service.
Give me the strength never to disown the poor or bend
my knees before insolent might.
Give me the strength to raise my mind high above daily
trifles.
And give me the strength to surrender my strength to thy
will with love.

Rabindranath Tagore[2]

14

Sola's courage

We will have to repent in this generation not merely for the hateful words and actions of the bad people but for the appalling silence of the good people.

Martin Luther King in a letter from Birmingham Jail in the States

Ours is a long and often silent struggle. Why do we struggle? Two reasons: we struggle because we love and not because we hate, and we struggle because our faith in God is alive, not dead.

Marta Torres, freedom-fighter and peace activist

Mr Minister, we must remind you that you are not God. You are just a man. And one day your name shall be merely a faint scribble on the pages of history, while the name of Jesus Christ, the Lord of the Church, shall live forever.

Desmond Tutu, speaking to South Africa's former Minister of Law and Order

Sola Sierra was not known in Britain, but in her native Chile many regarded her as an inspirational voice for truth. She died of a heart attack, in 1999, at the age of 63. I regard her as one of the many truly courageous women of the twentieth century. Sola devoted her life and indomitable energy to the cause of justice and human rights in her country. She was a simple woman, whose character grew with time and circumstances, who taught herself all she knew and, by the end, had a truly extraordinary determination and character.

Sola was born in San Miguel. She told her story of why her mother called her Sola which means 'Alone'. 'She had to go through labour alone. When my father eventually arrived, she told him: "My daughter came into the world all on her own." So she called me Sola Angela. I didn't realise how my life was destined to bear out my name.' The aptness of her name surfaced again years later when the musician Sting composed a song for Sola and the other relatives of the 'disappeared ones': 'They Dance Alone'.

During the presidency of Salvador Allende, Sola worked tirelessly among the poor in Santiago and other cities, promoting community health activities. In 1976, under the Government of General Pinochet, her husband was taken away because of his work as a union leader in the construction industry, and was never seen again.

Sola's response to Waldo's disappearance was to become active in the organisation, which had been set up by the Roman Catholic church, supporting relatives of those who had either been detained or lost. Despite continuing danger, this group pressed throughout the 1980s for information on the several thousand Chileans who had disappeared, and for those who had committed human rights crimes to be brought to justice. Even after Pinochet left office, Sola and other relatives were not given any information about their loved ones.

In time, she became president of the organisation, insisting that reconciliation was a task for everyone: 'I believe in national reconciliation, but only if there are gestures and deeds which show that everyone wants it. Sometimes, when there is talk of national reconciliation, what is meant is that the families of the victims have to do all the reconciling.' Throughout these years, Sola and her friends often seemed to be 'dancing alone' as they sought for lasting justice in Chile.

Towards the end of her life, still working as a fearless campaigner for human rights, Sola was immensely hopeful that the truth about thousands of Chilean women, children and men who had disappeared, would come out. She felt that her efforts had not been in vain, although she never discovered her husband's fate. She told friends that the voices of the disappeared would ultimately not be silenced, even if they had been for so long.

Whatever else may be said about Sola's life, her sheer courage in the face of enormous threats over many years stands out. Her bravery was part and parcel of her spirituality. She was determined to discover what had happened to the 'disappeared ones' throughout Chile, and nothing deterred her fight for basic justice. Often, as she herself said, she stood alone or with only a few friends. She became, as many in Chile recognized, a woman not only of determination but also of warmth, compassion and insight; a charismatic and inspirational voice amidst violence, untruth and persecution.

Most of us are not placed in such a situation. Our lives, at least outwardly, move in calmer currents. We live with a 'sense of security' which was denied to Sola and to many others in the world. Yet I believe that her courageous struggles can widen our own spiritual horizons and enlarge our capacities for compassion, locally and at a global level.

People like Sola take us out of our fragile securities, and reveal the truth that our lives are actually lived out on a wider canvas. Her vision also raises a personal question: what greater potential do I carry in my own life that may remain hidden?

And when I remember Sola, I also think of her companions, many of whom still fight for justice in Chile. The relatives of 'the disappeared' who hope, pray and struggle for that day when justice will dawn and truth will emerge. They, like Sola, believe that day is coming. Their faithfulness will be rewarded.

It was your courage
that inspired us, Sola;
your bravery in the face
of threats,
of endless harassments,
of daily personal danger.

You did not sit at home
as others
suffered brutal injustice;
you were not silent
when human rights
were abused;
you gave voice to
'the disappeared'
all over your land.

You never gave up,
or lost hope,
or became cynical.

Sola's courage

You pressed on
in your fight for truth,
and through your witness
God has revealed
a little more of Herself
to us.

15

Antonio's magic

I try and tell them that the most wonderful thing in the world is to be who you are. That to be black is to shine and aim high.

Leoniyene Price, United States

We make our lives so hectic that we eliminate the slightest risk of looking into ourselves. Even the idea of meditation can scare people. They fear looking into their hearts lest it be like being thrown out of the door of a spaceship to float forever in a dark, chilling void. Nothing could be further from the truth. But in a world dedicated to distraction, silence and stillness terrify us. Looking into the nature of our mind is the last thing we would dare to do. And sometimes even when the cell door on our heart is flung open, we choose not to escape and find freedom.

Sogyal Rinpoche, monk and teacher[1]

In 1964, Jean Vanier, a Canadian, after many years of studying and teaching philosophy and theology, bought a house in Trosy-Breuil in France. He invited two men with intellectual disabilities to live with him. He named the house L'Arche, after Noah's ark – both a place of refuge and of new beginnings.

L'Arche is now a network of more than one hundred communities in thirty countries, inhabited by people with disabilities and their care-givers. Their goal is to achieve a sense of community and dignity not possible within an institution.

For many years, I had the privilege of being associated with a small L'Arche community in South India. It was called Asha Niketan ('place of hope') and from those who lived there I learned so much about my own humanity. I discovered, through the lives of my intellectually handicapped friends, a world of challenge, beauty, simplicity and goodness. Without words, or with just a few words, they taught me much about God, about human relationships, about the meaning of love. I saw Jesus in them – sometimes a Jesus who was in agony and suffering.

In saying this, I also recognize the violence, anger and despair which accompanies profound intellectual disability. It is sometimes far from easy to live alongside those who are handicapped intellectually. Yet at Asha Niketan, I was taught by my friends about the immense value attached to qualities of the heart as distinct from those of the mind. At the level of the life of grace and faith they took me on a new journey.

In a beautiful passage, Jean Vanier speaks of this 'way of the heart' as it was revealed to him by Antonio who lives in one of the L'Arche communities:

First, let me tell you about Antonio, who has brought many people into the way of the heart. Antonio came to our community in Trosly when he was twenty years old, after many years in hospital. He could not walk, speak, or use his hands; he needed extra oxygen to breathe. He was a weak and fragile man in many ways but he had an

incredible smile and beautiful shining eyes. There was no
anger or depression in him. That is not to say that he
didn't get annoyed from time to time, especially if his
bathwater was too hot or too cold or if the assistants
forgot about him! What is important is that he had
accepted his limits and disabilities; he had accepted
himself just as he was. Antonio could not love by being
generous, by giving things to people or by doing things
for them; he himself was too needy. He lived a life of
trust. In this way, he touched many people's hearts.
When one loves with trust, one does not give things, one
gives oneself and, so, calls forth a communion of hearts.
Antonio touched and awakened the hearts of many
assistants who came to live in his house. He led them
into the way of the heart. Often, they would tell me so,
in words to this effect: 'Antonio has changed my life. He
led me out of a society of competition where one has
to be strong and aggressive into a world of tenderness
and mutuality, where each person, strong or weak, can
exercise their gifts.'

Jean Vanier[2]

Christ of the vulnerable,
thank you
for revealing this
'way of the heart'
through Antonio
and many other
women, children and men
who are
intellectually handicapped.

With our
over-burdened minds
and atrophied hearts
we sometimes forget
the many things
that You are teaching us
through the wisdom
and beauty
of their lives.

16

The stonecutters' struggles

Sholinghur is an old weaving and market town in southern India. It has been a place of human settlement for thousands of years and has been part of different kingdoms down through these long centuries. High above the crowded town, approached by a thousand magnificently carved stone steps, stands an ancient Hindu temple – a place of pilgrimage for thousands of devotees every year. From the precincts of this place of prayer, one looks down across the plains where green paddy fields (thanks to electricity and pump sets) alternate with vast tracks of thorny scrub – the home of hundreds of wandering animals such as goats and sheep, cows and water buffalo. In the wet season, in a hundred fields, bullocks plough in preparation for the rice planting – part of the timeless cycle of rural India. To see these bullocks at work, against the backcloth of tall palmyra trees, is to witness a scene unchanged in centuries.

In years gone by, many of the roads surrounding Sholinghur were only narrow sandy tracks – an unmapped maze of lanes reaching out across these seemingly limitless plains. But now things have changed and the town can be reached by fairly good tar-sealed roads. The road from Sholinghur to the neighbouring town of Pallipet is busy with regular buses, some private cars, many lorries, thousands of cycles and the ubiquitous bullock carts. And it is by the side of this road that a community of stonecutters live and work. The community must have one of the least enviable jobs in the world. Day after day, they cut rocks from the granite hillside and then, by hand, break these huge boulders into smaller stones. They then load these stones into lorries which carry them to different parts of Tamil Nadu.

To say that the lives of these stonecutters is hard is an understatement. Their life is exceptionally hard; they are appallingly exploited and oppressed; their living conditions are terrible and it will take at least another generation to free these workers from this dreadful bondage. Their daily working conditions are unspeakable – hewing granite in temperatures which are usually between 85°F and 105°F – the heat coming off the hill face is always intense, with very little seasonal change. The actual breaking of the stones, by men, women and children with small hammers, is a job which would kill most people within weeks.

The stonecutters live in small communities – perhaps up to 30 families in one place, and it may take them several years to 'work' the hillside. At night, they shelter in fragile thatched huts, more like thatched tents than the traditional sturdy mud and thatch huts of rural India. These tiny homes cling precariously to the hill slope. There is no water available, and the mothers walk a kilometre to find even a single drop. What must it be like to come back after a day amidst the stones and then search for a pot of water for washing and cooking? Once a week, a group from the community go to Sholinghur bazaar for rice.

The hillside itself is owned by the Tamil Nadu government, but the granite areas are let out to various 'owners' who are absolute landlords. These bosses are totally ruthless as far as the workforce is concerned and even today, at the end of the twentieth century, they pay a tiny amount for a full lorry of broken stones. If they are 'fortunate' (hardly an appropriate word in such a context), the family, as a whole, takes back around £1 at the end of a day's labour. If they are lucky. Often it is less. The hold which these owners have over the workers is complete, because through the years they have loaned money to them, and this financial obligation creates a kind of cementing of the bondage – a sad reality everywhere in the developing world. From what I have seen of these situations, there appears to be no humanity at all on the part of the 'owners'. The dark satanic mills of Victorian England seem, in comparison with this situation, like paradise.

Because they regard themselves as a nomadic group, none of the children go to the local Government school in Sholinghur. The parents prefer the children to work on the hillside, ensuring a little more daily income. Most of the children work hard, helping to break and carry the stones, and the infants sit close by their mothers on a boiling hot pile of stones. It is little wonder that all kinds of illnesses are found in the stonecutters' community, not least among the children, many of whom die at an early age.

Recently in some areas of South India, development workers have tried to fight along with the stonecutters for their basic rights. In a society where millions live below the official poverty line, this is not an easy task and very little headway has been made in such places like Sholinghur where oppression reigns. The injustice is so deep and the bondage so pervasive that it is difficult to know where to enter this whole cycle of deprivation. An obvious solution would be to create stone-workers co-operatives, but the formation of such co-operatives in this part of the world faces all kinds of official, bureaucratic restrictions. Nor are such groups given encouragement by Government departments.

At Sholinghur, some local Christians have started a small informal 'evening school' for the stonecutters' children. Many of the parents, all of whom are illiterate, join in drawing the Tamil alphabet on the sand. The fact that some outside people care about their plight seems to be just as important as any formal learning – a lesson which is often lost sight of in the million dollar 'development schemes' which come from the drafting committees of the World Bank and many others.

If there was an easy answer to the situation of the stone-workers on the Pallipet Road, such groups would not be in the terrible plight which they face. There are no easy solutions, and among certain groups in India today, exploitation is increasing, though in other communities the fight for justice has brought benefits. Despite the dreadful plight of these particular stone-workers, the situation in rural India is not static, and awareness about basic human rights is growing.

I can never forget the little community on the road just beyond Sholinghur. In that dry and rocky place, amidst these fragile houses, you will find families who must be among the most exploited in India. They seem to be totally powerless, and even their fight for water seems only to bring them more oppression. But as we look into the tired faces of the stonecutters, we find laughter, intelligence, hope and deep compassion. These people are alive to life perhaps much more than I will ever be. And through them, God offers an amazing gift – the uprooting of my easy assumptions about my own priorities.

17

Tom's faith

Dear Peter,

One of the things we discussed when we met was the kind of language we use to express our belief in God. For me, traditional religious language is not always easy to take on board! I enclose a personal creed. Lots more could be said, but it is a starting point. Let me know what you think about it.

I believe in
  – human vulnerability and fallibility.
  – the determination to survive and to flourish to the
      end of earthly life.
  – the paradox between self-centred survival and
      compassionate gentleness.
  – the deep patterns of transformation, of new growing
      from old.
  – the paradoxical power of the small and weak over
      the large and strong; of quality over quantity.
  – the power of love to triumph over suffering.
  – human solidarity, and relationships, reflecting
      (and capable of going beyond) the mysterious
      patterns of connectedness and inter-dependence in
      nature.
  – an inner life with responses to promptings;

with hidden energies, resources and liberations;
with yearnings and visions for harmony in relationships
   rising above self service;
with urges to search, to question, to find out,
   to play a meaningful part, to celebrate.

For me,
   all this is found in my God's fingerprints,
   all reflect God's nature
   all are found in God
      totally integrated with the created·order and the
        human condition,
      in God's footprints on this visited planet.

Thanks for reading it all.
Be in touch.

      Tom

18

Mary and Thomas

If life has taught me nothing else, it has shown that God is truly a God of surprises! I am attracted to such a God because you never know what a new day will bring. And it seems that the more you open yourself to God, the more surprises there are in store.

A few years ago, one of God's surprising moves brought a small family to our front door in Chennai (Madras) in South India. It was late in the evening and much of the city was flooded as the monsoon rain had been torrential for days on end. A hurricane was on the cards. This is what I wrote in my diary the following day :

Today is December 3rd, but in a surprising and totally unexpected way Christmas arrived on our doorstep last night. It happened like this. In unbelievably torrential monsoon rain an unknown family arrived. All of them were in a sorry state and the two tiny children (one about two and the other only four months old) were literally dying before our eyes. None of them had eaten for days.

And because it was so wet, their situation seemed a hundred times worse than it would have been in the dry season. We took them all in, gave them some food and medicine and fixed up a room for them. At least it was dry, and if nothing else they were out of reach of the lashing monsoon. Together we all lit a kerosene lamp and within minutes the room had the semblance of a warm home.

As Mary and Thomas (our friends of the night) shared their story of homelessness, unemployment and gut-wrenching poverty, I thought of all the families around us in this city who would be in a similar plight. These families, out on the pavements with their fragile thatched homes washed away, still had to face the relentless monsoon. At least Mary and Thomas had found a temporary shelter from the storm.

Today the children look much better, and the parents have slept well. Tomorrow we hope to be able to get some work for Thomas which will bring in a few rupees. Yet their long-term future, as for millions of other families in India, is uncertain. Will the children live long enough to become teenagers? Will the parents find permanent work and some basic shelter? I find these questions rotating endlessly in my head the longer I live in this beautiful but poverty-stricken land.

Very early this morning, these words came to me, for Mary and Thomas have so much to teach me; to teach all of us who make 'security' a top priority:

Lord, a long time ago Job wondered
   why so many ills had come his way.
   He felt that life had been hard and unfair.

But, Lord, I think I have a different question
   to ask you.
   I don't know quite how to ask it, but I'll try.

Lord, why have so many good things come my way?
Why is it that I have so much?
Health, a job, a loving family . . .
The list seems endless.

And as I think about all these riches,
I remember this evening with Mary and Thomas
and their two babies.
They are absolutely starving;
they have nothing, except each other.
Even the poor health they had
seems to be draining away.

Lord, I asked you that question.
But when I think about it,
it is not so much a question that I want to ask you –
rather a request.
I don't know how to put it but I'll try –
it goes something like this –
'Lord Jesus, could you somehow give me
a heart
that
cares more?
And not just when a family in distress
comes to our door.'

19

Mahala's gift

Slowly, as the years go by, I learn about the importance of powerlessness. I experience it in my own life
and I live with it in my work. The secret is not to be
afraid of it – not to run away. The dying know we are
not God. They accept that we cannot halt the process
of cancer, the inexorable march of that terrible army
that takes over the human body like an occupying
force, pillaging, raping, desecrating without respect
and without quarter. All they ask is that we do not
desert them: that we stand our ground at the foot of
the cross. At this stage of the journey, of being there,
of simply being: it is, in many ways, the hardest part.

Sheila Cassidy, doctor and writer[1]

As a spectacularly radiant dawn broke over the Sound of
Iona, Mahala moved quietly on into the next part of her
pilgrimage. For her a new day was truly breaking and a
new understanding of God's purpose was unfolding. During
the last hours of her life, as I sat with friends by her bedside, I had pondered on her seemingly limitless creativity
and remarkable intelligence. Now that lively spirit had
gone from our midst, and we shared in a deep silence as we
gave thanks, in our own ways, for her life.

Some weeks earlier, Mahala had returned to her home close to the shore on Iona to spend her remaining days beside its swift-flowing tides. Her earlier plans were no longer possible. As an internationally renowned expert in fossils, she had hoped to continue her research work, write books and become part and parcel of the village life of Iona. It was not to be. Cancer was diagnosed and the final stages of her illness came swiftly.

A few moments after her peaceful passing, we pulled back the curtains in her bedroom where she had spent her last days. The brilliance of the morning illumined the whole room, and the peace-filled body which lay on the bed. At that moment I did not think of Mahala's incompleted plans, but rather of God's presence enfolding all of us in that room – the dead and the living. We were, as one, in God's embrace. The day ahead for us who mourned would be very different from Mahala's new day, yet in the mystery of God's compassion we were held together; connected by invisible, yet almost tangible, threads to the One who had created us all.

Running through my head were the words of a prayer which I had heard not only on Iona but in many places:

> Bless to us, O God,
> The morning sun that is above us,
> The good earth that is beneath us,
> The friends that are around us,
> Your image deep within us,
> The day which is before us.

Contemporary society, for the most part, does not deal well with the process of dying, although there are notable exceptions such as the hospice movement where death's multiple dimensions are addressed with seriousness, hope and laughter. For the most part, we are scared of the process: frightened by the thought of such an uncharted journey. Will we be screaming with pain at the last moments? Will we have a friend or a loved one near us? Will we be at home or in hospital? Will our death be sudden and brutal like so many deaths in our world? Many questions. And only fragmentary answers.

Yet on that glorious morning as Mahala slipped from our sight, I felt that all of us are held in a much wider frame of meaning than we can ever dream of or imagine. In this earthly part of our journey we can only discern a tiny part of the Creator's purpose – and perhaps that truth comes home to us with fresh clarity as we sojourn with the dying. The questions remain – as does the pilgrimage, which is why these Indian words have such prophetic depth:

> Living Lord,
> from the unreal lead me to the real;
> from darkness lead me to the light;
> from death lead me to immortality.

20

Nguyen Vu's open heart

God invites us today to re-define prophesy; that voice of truth which often comes from outside the temple. The world's next revolution will be a religious one, but not in a sectarian way. It is a revolution just waiting to be touched and tapped.

Vincent Donovan, priest and friend of the poor

Nguyen Vu was born in Viet Nam. He is now a medical student in the United States and recently wrote me a very special letter which I see as a parable of our times. The first part of the letter concerned an elderly sick woman who had come to Nguyen Vu's hospital with her young grand-daughter who was suffering from abdominal pain. It went on:

After I had informed the young girl that we would need a pregnancy test, there came a long silence. She looked down at the floor uncomfortably. At last the elderly woman let out a long sigh and spoke in a tremulous voice: 'I have been "mother" to her and her sister since they were born. I'm seventy-one and can't keep up any more. My sugar problem is bad, and I have not eaten since early morning.' I stood there listening quietly and realised that good medicine in this context would have to go beyond a sound diagnosis or a quick glucose source for the grandmother.

Vignettes like this one have been my daily nourishment throughout the first three years of my medical training. They remind me of verses from the Shaker hymn, 'Simple Gifts'. As I stood by the patient's bedside that evening, I felt an elementary love for the person in front of me and a deep connection to my own history. Long before I discerned my calling to be a physician, I learned my lessons about poverty, hardship, violence and injustice from post-war Viet Nam.

While my father was in a Communist concentration camp, the rest of my family sought survival on a government rubber plantation. Before I knew my multiplication tables, I learned to work with my grandfather and earned a few extra kilos of corn working on neighbouring farms. Before I had any conception of parasites or bacteria, I saw malnourished children dropping out of school to sell newspapers or scavenge in large rubbish dumps. I saw my mother shivering helplessly from malarial fevers, and my grandfather wasting from TB.

When my father was released from concentration camp, our family escaped on a wooden boat which he had made. We were amongst the thousands of families who fled Viet Nam in search of hope and dignity. We lived through the monsoon storms of the South China Sea; we survived turbulent months in refugee camps and early years of settlement in the United States. After all this, three greatest gifts have remained with me: life itself, a soul that can remember and a heart that can feel.

Throughout the years of my formal education and medical school, I have searched for ways to forge meanings from my childhood experiences. It has led me to meet and work with children from American inner cities and from the former Soviet-block countries. This search has taken me to leprosy villages in India and inside refugee camps where my family once lived. In those places and by the patient's bedside, I sense the pieces of my past and future lives converging. I still have a strong 'feeling heart', and am grateful that I can give back something to others, as an expression of gratitude for life and all its 'simple gifts'.

> Christ of every pilgrim heart,
> I thank you
> for Nguyen Vu's journey,
> and for all
> who have travelled
> on
> a similar path
> in our interconnected world.
>
> Help me,
> in my own way,
> to be able
> to thank you
> for these
> priceless gifts:
>
> life itself,
> a soul that remembers
> and
> a feeling heart.

21

Sara's justified anger

The greatest religious problem today is how to be both a mystic and a militant; in other words, how to combine the search for an expansion of inner awareness with effective social action, and how to feel one's true identity in both.

Ursula King, homemaker and writer

One of the most exciting aspects of non-violence is that it calls forth all our creativity and imagination, all our reserves of individuality, uniqueness, courage and humour. I don't believe we have even begun to imagine the extent of the upside-down world we are called to live in. We have become so familiar with the gospel stories that we forget how utterly shocking, radical and different Jesus' lifestyle was.

Helen Steven, visionary, peace activist

Greenham Common. The name brings home to us the memory of countless courageous women who participated in the long vigil against the cruise missile base which had been established there in the 1980s. One of those who committed herself to this non-violent demonstration was a member of the Quaker Women's Group. Sara's words, although written some years ago, speak to us with fresh urgency not just about nuclear warheads but about the increasing global violence which is a marker of our time. Can we re-visit the way of non-violent action and relearn from its wisdom?

Waiting, watching, witnessing, women at the Greenham fence, present as the death of the planet is rehearsed by people acting in our name, the death of thousands of unknown women who live at a distance, in a country where men practise our death. I stood at the fence one night in September, feet rooted to the muddy ground, hands deep in my pockets, watching through the wire that flat ravaged land that is now never dark, never quiet, imagining through the fence a field of bracken and scrub, a field of flowers, a field of corn, a field of children playing.

Red police car, blue lights flashing, 'What are you doing, then, love? Not cutting the fence are you?' 'No, just praying at it.' A soldier with a dog walks up and down inside, suspicious, watching me watching him. 'Good evening.' 'Good evening.' I wait, not knowing what I am waiting for. The kingdoms of the Lord? A hundred yards to my left, women cut the wire, roll away the stone, and walk into the tomb. No angels greet them; no resurrection yet.

Yet still women witness to that possibility, the possibility that something may be accomplished which in our own strength we cannot do. Women waiting, watching, just being there, behaving as if peace were possible, living our dream of the future now. 'Why do you come here? Why do you keep coming?' – a soldier near Emerald camp on an earlier visit – 'It's no use, there's nothing you can do, what do you women think you can do by coming here? The missiles are here, you won't change anything, why do you come?'

We come to watch, we come to witness, we come with our hands full of ribbon and wool, flowers and photos of loved ones, hands full of poems and statements and prayers, hands full of hope and the knowledge that such hope is impossible to rational minds. I come to be with the women who live here, the dykes, the dropouts, the mothers and grandmothers, angels with countenances like lightning, I come to talk with the police, the soldiers, men who might be gardeners standing by the tomb; I come to meet Christ in them.[1]

22

Phoebe, Anna and Diana's hopes

I long for compassion to be the hallmark of our society –
I long to see men honouring women and women
    honouring men –
I long to see gentleness, tenderness and integrity in
    relationships
between sexes, and between races and people of all ages.

Pippa, homemaker

We have to realise that a creative being lives within
    ourselves,
whether we like it or not, and that we must get out of
    its way,
for it will give us no peace until we do so.

Mary Richards[1]

Each of these women has inspired me in different ways, and I regard their voices as prophetic ones. Phoebe has died, but her vision lives on in the minds and hearts of countless others. Anna has known first-hand the struggles and joys of her own people, and has been able to articulate in a powerful way the living spirituality of Brazilian people. Diana, who works in the States, continues to be a bridge-builder among the great and varied religious traditions of the world.

Phoebe, Anna and Diana's hopes

Dear God,
make a full and complete woman of me,
not an also-ran or a pale reflection of a man
included in that word: 'man'.
The men say, 'Jesus died for us men and for our
    salvation'
as if I were part of a package deal,
part of his household, his luggage:
but I know I am not just a part of his equipment to be a
    person.
I am an other, quite different person.
I have my own name,
my own personality.
I am feminine
and that is quite different from being masculine.

*Phoebe Willetts, visionary, turbulent priest,
advocate of nuclear disarmament*[2]

In this moment I humbly want to be the voice of Black women and men, Indian women and men, as well as white women and men in Latin America. Indian, Black people and women have been oppressed and marginalized. But we resist; we keep on living and hoping. We women ask how? Black people ask the same question. After centuries of suffering we keep on living, suffering but laughing because life is a celebration.

What strength sustains this attitude? Where does it come from? Well it is something very strong which comes from deep inside and this strength is spirituality. Spirituality is what keeps us living and giving hope and meaning to life. That's a commonality we people from the Third World countries have been experiencing – a cry for life, a scream for life. Spirituality is lived in the midst of the struggles, in the small signs of life which enable us to 'feast' life. In Brazil, we cannot understand spirituality without the 'fiesta', the gracious moment when we communicate with God who is 'graciousness'.

Anna Maria Tepdino, teacher in Rio de Janeiro, Brazil

Our religious traditions are more like rivers than monuments. They are not static and they are not over. They are still rolling with forks and confluences, rapids and waterfalls. Where these rivers of faith flow depends on who we are and who we become. I am a Christian in a world of many faiths. I have travelled the path with Hindus and Buddhists, Muslims and Jews, Jains, Sikhs and Native Americans and these encounters have challenged, changed and deepened my own faith. As a rabbi friend once put it: 'It is dialogue with one another, or death.'

Diana Eck, student, scholar, teacher[3]

Story-telling God,
help us to bring our own stories
to one another.
Our stories of
  hope
  shame
  disappointment
  clowning
  false turnings
  success
  embarrassments
  desire
  empty roads

Phoebe, Anna and Diana's hopes

frustration
commitment
stupidity
and love against the odds,
And to see in their telling,
Your spirit at work
in the ebb and flow
of our daily lives.

23

Sue's psalm

Sue and John are close friends who live in Nottingham. Sue works as a doctor in the inner city and John is vicar of a large parish near the city centre. They radiate compassion. In recent times, John has been battling with cancer. At one point when he was extremely low, Sue wrote her own psalm for John, her family and the wider world. Her psalm was based on Psalm 77 and describes both a personal situation and a global one. It springs from the heart of an individual who works at the coalface, and who embodies in her life a joyful and profound faithfulness to God's calling.

> Lord, the future is so uncertain
> and I don't know if I can bear it;
> the health of my dearest love is in the balance.
> I cry for his suffering.
> Take away his sickness,
> preserve and keep my family
> in good health for many years.
> Let him accomplish
> the work set before him;
> do not take him:
> his children need him.
> I am troubled

but know that you are near
and comforting me.
Give me strength,
and let me live in hope.

The world is full of your love, O God;
people who know you and do not know you
do good things.
Blessings abound,
as do opportunities
to share in your work of love.
The wonder of creation,
demonstrates your power and glory.
May the world
see the needs of all peoples:
may the poor be lifted up,
and the rich see their riches
as gifts to be shared.
May justice fill the earth.

24

Christian's testament

Christian de Chergé was a Trappist monk. For some years he had been Superior of his monastery in Algiers and it was there in 1994, along with six other brothers, that he was murdered by local terrorists. What is remarkable about his last 'testament', which was only opened after his death, is his total solidarity with the communal agony in Algeria and his unwillingness to be thought of as a martyr. He wanted it known that his death was only one among many others, and that his killers were also bearers of God's image, open to forgiveness like himself.

> If it should happen one day – and it could be today –
> that I become a victim of the terrorism which now seems ready
> to encompass all the foreigners living in Algeria,
> I would like my community, my Church, my family,
> to remember that my life was *given* to God and to this country.
> I ask them to accept that the One Master of all life
> was not a stranger to this brutal departure.
> I ask them to pray for me:
> for how could I be found worthy of such an offering?
> I ask them to be able to associate such a death with the many other deaths

which were just as violent, but forgotten through
    indifference
and anonymity.
My life has no more value than any other.
Nor any less value.
In any case, it has not the innocence of childhood.
I have lived long enough to know that I share in the evil
which seems, alas, to prevail in the world,
even in that which would strike me blindly.
I should like, when the time comes, to have a clear
    space
which would allow me to beg forgiveness of God
and of all my fellow human beings,
and at the same time to forgive with all my heart the
    one who would
strike me down.
    I could not desire such a death.
    It seems to me important to state this.
I do not see, in fact, how I could rejoice
if this people I love were to be accused indiscriminately
    of my murder.

25

Healing

We come to you,
Healer and Friend;
you who understand us
so much better than we understand ourselves;
you come
to permeate our human condition;
to walk with the bruised people and places
of our time;
to enfold the wounded and the weary;
to offer us an inner springtime.
Your song pierces
even our darkest days,
and you accompany us
when our bodies are racked with pain,
when our minds are in confusion,
when our self-esteem is lost,
when our failures overwhelm,
when our faith falters,
when our relationships break down,
when in our loneliness
we move beyond our tears
and know the agony of abandonment.

On page after page in the Gospels we read of that relationship between Jesus and sick people. Christ's healing took place on many levels of mind and body, for he was concerned with a life of wholeness. Through his ministry, the healing touch of divine love and forgiveness reached into the deepest places of people's lives. Even to touch the hem of Christ's garments was seen as a movement towards healing. To paraphrase some words of Eddie Askew of The Leprosy Mission, in Christ was an assurance, however high the waves; a strength, however high the tides. In Jesus the burdens of the human heart were transfigured.

In Iona Abbey every Tuesday evening there is a service of prayers for healing and, at a later point in the liturgy, a time when people can both receive and offer the laying on of hands. Large numbers of prayer requests reach Iona, and these may be for individuals, families, communities and even countries. The requests may also be for creation itself, now groaning under the weight of pollution and other environmentally destructive forces.

Prior to this particular service, those who are staying as guests with the Iona Community on the island have an opportunity to discuss the whole question of Christian healing. I have had the privilege of sharing in many of these reflections, and I have learned a great deal from them. Some people are very aware of Christ's healing power at work in their lives, others are confused and uncertain about the whole subject, while a great number are open to exploring the various issues around healing either in ourselves or for the wider world. In these sessions, there are always questions around whether or not we are talking about 'physical healing' or 'healing in general', and many wonder whether healing only takes place when we have a deep, personal faith in Jesus Christ.

In my own understanding, I see Christ as 'the world's

healer' – enfolding all of us in his care. One member of the
Iona Community, Anna Briggs, has expressed this truth in
a wonderfully imaginative way in one of her hymns which
is now sung throughout the world church. Anna's insights
open our minds to a Christ who permeates every facet of
our human condition with healing energies through the
work of the Holy Spirit.

> We lay our broken world
> in sorrow at your feet
> haunted by hunger, war and fear,
> oppressed by power and hate.
>
> We bring our broken selves,
> confused and closed and tired;
> then through your gift of healing grace,
> new purpose is inspired.
>
> O Spirit, on us breathe,
> with life and strength anew;
> find in us love, and hope and trust,
> and lift us up to you.
>
> *Anna Briggs*[1]

It is to this healing power that we come with our own
wounds, pains and weakness, and also with the cries of our
sisters and brothers and of earth itself. Often with sorrow
in our hearts, as Anna's hymn reminds us, we lay our
burdens at the feet of Christ, who has himself walked the
road of suffering. Through our prayers we are not seeking
'to change God' but rather to open ourselves to the possibility that God's healing energy can flow within us.
Inviting the Holy Spirit to breathe on us: to bring healing to
our troubled hearts and sick bodies.

In one modern translation of Psalm 42, we read: 'I want to drink deep draughts of God: I am thirsty for God-alive.' These words of longing echo the feelings in the heart of the woman who met Jesus having had severe bleeding for twelve years (Luke 8:40–48). She believed that if only she could touch his clothes, healing would follow. Eventually, through the crowd, she was able to touch the edge of his cloak, and at once her bleeding stopped. The Gospel narrative continues:

> Jesus asked : 'Who touched me?' Everyone denied it, and Peter said, 'Master, the people are all around you and crowding in on you.' But Jesus said, 'Someone touched me, for I knew it when the power went out of me.' The woman saw that she had been found out, so she came trembling and threw herself at Jesus' feet. There in front of everybody, she told him why she had touched him, and how she had been healed at once. Jesus said to her, 'My daughter, your faith has made you well, go in peace.'

She approached Jesus with faith that healing would occur: that some kind of transformation would take place in her life that day. And it did. She went home, a healed person. Apart from that we know few details of her life, but what shines through is the conviction in this person, that her God was a healing God.

I believe we can say with conviction that 'God heals' which is a very different thing from saying that God answers all our prayers in exactly the way we want! That does not happen, for God comes to us in every situation in his own way: surprisingly, challengingly, disturbingly. And so it is not a contradiction to say that we may experience deep inner healing while remaining seriously ill.

Maureen was a person of prayer. Just a few days before her death in a hospice we were talking together, and she said to me: 'When you get home read verses five to seven in Psalm 84 for they describe exactly how I feel.' What the Psalmist had written there was this: 'How happy are those whose strength comes from You; as they pass through the dry valley it becomes a place of springs, and they grow stronger as they go.' Although terminally ill, Maureen at her death was a healed woman: an individual at peace with herself, with her loved ones, with her God. Her cancer had not disappeared, but she had discovered dimensions of God's healing power which transformed her life. Or to put it another way: she had been made whole in Christ's healing love.

My pastoral work has convinced me that God's healing is a mystery and yet something which is very real. And it is not only about that healing which takes place in the lives of people. It has, for me, a much wider reference, for the whole world is a place of God's creative work. That is why it is so important to seek God's healing in areas of conflict and of hatred, whether in families or in nations. Reconciliation, in its many faces, is profoundly a work of healing; of God's light infusing the darkness of bitterness and violence. And similarly, God's healing activity connects to those contemporary prayers for our burning forests, our polluted rivers, our rape of the earth.

As I start to recognize this vast canvas of God's healing activity, I begin to understand a little of what the Psalmist meant when he said: 'O Lord, I will always sing of your constant love: I will proclaim your faithfulness for ever. I know that your love will last for all time, that your faithfulness is as permanent as the sky.' (Psalm 89:1–2). This means to me that there is an ever-flowing stream of our Creator's healing energy moving through human life and through all of creation. We touch into this healing force, and when we experience its activity we can sing with the Israelites: 'The LORD is my shepherd; I have everything I need. He gives me new strength; even if I go through the deepest darkness, I will not be afraid, for you are with me' (Psalm 23:1–4).

All of this is not to imply that I don't have many questions around this whole issue of God's healing work. Certain aspects of Christian healing make me deeply uncomfortable, and I am very suspicious of some folk who claim great 'healing powers' which they claim have come from Christ. But I do know this. In some of my darkest hours, and there have been plenty of them, I have experienced Christ's enfolding love, reassuring me that a new dawn will break and that peace will come to my soul. It is this quiet testimony, which I know is shared by millions of my sisters and brothers, that enables me to write, with sincerity, a prayer such as this:

> Spirit of the living Christ,
> even in our darkest moments;
> in the searchings of our mind,
> in the longing of our heart,
> in the pains of our body,
> we thirst for your presence.
> And all around,
> the broken people and places
> of our planet
> also thirst for you.
> Enlarge our vision,
> calm our hearts,
> and walk with all who travel the road
> of our world's suffering and pain.

Waymarks

Watch now, dear Lord, with those who wake or watch
   or weep tonight,
and give your angels charge over those who sleep.
Tend your sick ones, O Lord Christ, rest your weary
   ones,
bless your dying ones, soothe your suffering ones,
pity your afflicted ones, shield your joyous ones,
and all for your love's sake. Amen

St Augustine

26

Accepting life's unfinished symphonies

The theologian Karl Rahner spoke of the fact that most of life's symphonies remain unfinished. Many of our hopes never come to fruition. So much about our journey through life appears incomplete. In terms of our relationships, our health, our jobs and our friendships, there are always unfinished parts.

Sometimes it takes many years for us to recognize this essential incompleteness and when we do, we may feel resentment and disillusionment. Waves of frustration flow through our days. Somehow deep down – away beyond words and even thoughts – we had hoped for more. The intimacy that eluded us; the daughter that abandoned us; the job that became a total disaster area. And at one level or another we all experience something of this along life's path. The finished symphony just never happened.

Ronald Rolheiser, who is a spiritual guide for many of us, speaks clearly about the fact that such recognition of life's unfinished symphonies has to be mourned. It is a reality which elicits grief within us. He writes:

> When we fail to mourn properly our incomplete lives, then this incompleteness becomes a gnawing restlessness, a bitter centre, that robs our lives of delight.

Because we do not mourn, we demand that someone or something – a marriage partner, a sexual partner, an ideal family, having children, an achievement, a vocational goal, or a job – take all of our loneliness away. That, of course, is an unreal expectation which invariably leads to bitterness and disappointment. In this life, there is no finished symphony. We are built for eternity, Grand Canyons without a bottom. Because of that we will, this side of eternity, always be lonely, restless, incomplete – living in the torment of the insufficiency of everything attainable.

Ronald Rolheiser [1]

And such mourning can never be easy or superficial. Grief is a hard road and takes us to many places of great pain. Yet without mourning these lost symphonies in our lives can we ever move on? And the short answer is 'no', for we shall still endlessly seek the unattainable.

And here I am not writing about something abstract or academic. I've been there, like most other people. And like many whose friendships I value, I've wept profusely over my various unfinished agendas – and still do.

Yet I also believe that in some rather fragmentary way I have learned to mourn these unfinished parts of my life and move on. To leave them behind, and take on board at an emotional and spiritual level that many of my personal hopes, dreams and visions will never be fulfilled on this side of eternity. Rolheiser expressed that starkly when he wrote: 'Ultimately, we all sleep alone.'

And that fact when faced up to, and even partially accepted, can itself be the wellspring of fresh creativity within us. On the one side we will always be restless and lonely, carrying within our hearts many unfinished symphonies. On the other side, that very condition within our humanity can take us to spiritual depths which we may never have otherwise experienced. That I believe deeply, for I have seen the evidence of it in many lives.

In learning to mourn our unfinished symphonies and to move on, we discover an astonishing truth – at least I have! It is this. We may not have quite so many unfinished symphonies after all! In mourning them, we can place them in a wider perspective, and along the line be more gentle in the estimation of our lives. That does not mean that our lives are free of unfinished agendas, but it does suggest that we can place them within a broader frame of meaning. And maybe, after some time, we can truly celebrate the fact that 'we are as we are', human beings made in the image of a God who understands all of our longings and uprootedness much better than we do ourselves.

And all of this acceptance of incompleteness and the courage to move on is woven into a challenging prayer entitled 'Kiss Sleeping Beauty Goodbye' which was inspired by Madonna Kdbenschlag. Its words always propel me forward into new pilgrim paths:

> O God,
> I feel I have been
> Sleepwalking
> My way through life;
> Waiting in
> No woman's land
> For something significant to happen;
> For someone to come
> And lead me to
> The Real Life.

Alone
I have felt insignificant;
Unable to take control
Of my own life;
Not sure of what my life is.
Help me to wake up
And measure
My present realities;
Who I am
Where I am
And what I can be;
To kiss Sleeping Beauty goodbye
Once and for all
As I learn
To put my trust
In You.[2]

27

Valuing different sexualities

As I come to a mellow, even peaceful awareness
of my limited grasp of truth,
I don't need to defend myself
against people or experiences
which might hold new or challenging information.
I become open to these truths
that reside,
half-hidden, and often surprising,
in my own and others' journeys.
And this is a gift,
a rare treasure –
freeing me to understand
rather than to be understood;
calling me
to fewer words,
to awareness,
to humility,
to patience,
to laughter,
to tenderness,
to listening,
to dancing in the rain,
to waiting on that God
who always

welcomes home
a mellow heart.

In my pastoral experience, the issues around human sexuality arouse passion, pain and prejudice. Myriad voices within the contemporary debates on this issue claim our attention. They are not always gentle voices and can be overwhelmingly strident as people position themselves in relation to the hugely complex realities of sexual orientation and sexual behaviour.

In what we have erroneously called 'developed societies', we often grow up believing that we are each separate, isolated and alone. In such a climate we learn to live, consciously and unconsciously, with a range of internal fears – afraid that other people will hurt or misunderstand or totally reject us. Framed in this aloneness, we choose to believe in a world of separation in which we manage to privatize our lives, failing to recognize the amazingly rich and creative springs of life at work in 'the other'. We refuse to accept that which is a universal reality – 'difference'.

Thankfully, that is only part of the picture. The other part is that we are slowly awakening to the acceptance of 'difference' which includes among other things, our sexual orientation. For some, this is an incredibly tough learning process; for others a vibrant expression of maturity within our human journeying. One thing is certain. 'Acceptance of difference' can never be a neutral experience for it demands a substantial rearranging of our emotional and spiritual resources.

I have found that it sometimes feels like being at the foot of a great mountain when I suggest that in accepting a person's sexuality – genuinely accepting it, as opposed to agreeing to a vague idea that folk are different – we are acting normally! That we are not going mad, or acting strangely or going against the will of God.

As I read the Gospels, I am always struck by the fact that Jesus met people where they were in life. It may sound trite, but he saw their potential and valued their essential humanity, often in circumstances where other people only regarded them as walking disaster areas. And it is in this valuing of the human person that we can move into new depths of understanding, insight and awareness about one another, whatever our differences.

A prayer which is used in Iona Abbey includes the words: 'Lord, your image deep within us'. The image of God imprinted in the human person; every individual carrying those sparks of divinity which are markers of our Creator's energy and wisdom. I wonder if we believe that in a way which is healing for ourselves? In a way which enlarges our compassion and minimizes some of our internal fears, and our feelings of separation from 'the other'?

The journalist Andrew Sullivan, writing about his own experience as a gay man, reminded his readers of our inter-connected humanity, whatever our sexual orientation may be. They are words from his heart, but I feel sad that gay and lesbian people have still to remind others that they are first and foremost human beings.

> The homosexual's longings, his development, his dreams are human phenomena. They are, I think, instantly recognizable to any heterosexual, in their form if not their content. The humanity of homosexuals is clear everywhere. Perhaps nothing has illustrated this more clearly than the AIDS epidemic. Gay people have to confront grief and shock and mortality like anybody else. They die like all people die.[1]

Not very long ago, in Iona Abbey, the congregation cele-
brated sexual diversity in an exceptionally moving act of
worship. At the beginning of the service, I noticed that
some people were looking a bit uncomfortable with the
theme which was perhaps not quite what they expected.
They need not have feared. That summer evening in the
candle-lit quiet beauty of that magnificent place of prayer,
we shared in a liturgical act which must have lightened the
heart of God. It was a celebration grounded in a profoundly
prayerful interpretation of the Christian message.

I was not the only one in tears as various members of the
congregation shared their stories and offered prayers. This
was not some superficial propaganda exercise or a strident
attempt to make us aware of gay and lesbian issues. It was
a Christian community in prayer, seeking the guidance of
Christ, aware that we are all vulnerable and also strong
people. We asked God to help us accept one another in all
of our mystery, plurality and creativity.

As the service progressed, a gay friend reached over and
whispered that he had never felt more loved, accepted and
cherished. It was a sacred moment in God's house, for us
both. And it was a moment framed in Christ's accepting
love – that love which knows no boundaries or labels and
through which forgiveness flows.

Later that evening by the great St Martin's cross which
has stood close to the west door of Iona Abbey for over a
thousand years, a stranger spoke to me. He was on holiday
on the island and had wandered into the evening service.
We greeted one another and then he said: 'I came into
the church and when I realized what the service was
about I wanted to walk out. But I stayed on and I'm glad
I did. I want to thank your people for having the courage
to let it happen because it has changed me in a way I can't

figure out. I'll have a different outlook when I leave the island.'

Maybe for the first time in his life that visitor to Iona had to face up not only to the sexuality of others, but also to the movements in his own heart. I hope it was a start of a longer walk into appreciating and valuing sexual difference. And one day – maybe not too far into the future – we will abandon these easy labels which dominate our debates about human sexuality – and discover a basic truth: that we are one in Christ.

> God of compassion,
> you made us
> in your own image
> and our prayer is
> that each day you will
> illumine our minds,
> enlarge our awareness
> and
> free us from prejudice,
> so that we cease to
> marginalize,
> judge
> and condemn others
> because of their
> sexual orientation.
> And, along the way,
> help us to
> examine with honesty
> our own
> inner contradictions,
> sexual fears
> and emotional longings.

28

Suffering

Survivors, their voices choked with tears, their faces wrought with despair, tore at mangled steel and concrete, at shattered wooden and tin structures yesterday, to free loved ones after a massive earthquake rocked western Turkey, killing at least 2,000 people and wounding more than 11,000 others. Turkish officials feared the final death toll could reach 10,000.

Newspaper report, 18 August 1999

In the closing months of a century which had witnessed countless natural disasters, our world community shared in another one. This newspaper report suggests that up to 10,000 people had lost their lives. In fact, the figure was much greater – more than 40,000 died and around 200,000 were made homeless. Thousands of women, children and men were critically injured as the quake rocked villages, towns and cities during the middle of the night local time.

The first TV reports, hours after the disaster, said that around 200 people had been killed. It soon became 2,000, then a couple of days later 7,000. By the end of that first week, Turkish authorities were accepting that as many as tens of thousands of citizens had perished on that hot summer night. The scale of the disaster numbed the mind –

it was not possible to grasp in any intelligent way the numbers whose lives had either been taken or devastated.

Certainly this whole situation was far beyond my own imagining as I sat down to prepare a service for the following Sunday. What kind of God could allow this to happen, even if hundreds of buildings in the earthquake zone had been constructed without permits and with substandard materials? Why should these particular families be blown away in an instant? Was God there with them on that Tuesday night, or somewhere else? What does the Bible say about such overwhelming tragedy? And what of all the pain and accumulated grief left behind?

I read through some passages in Job. He was shouting in anger at God because he felt that he had been abandoned when troubles came to his life. He screams out, 'God has done this. He has set a trap to catch me. He has blocked the way, and I can't get through; he has hidden my path in darkness. He batters me from every side. He uproots my hope and leaves me to wither and die.' (Job 19:1–12). In the moment when he needed comfort and inner strength, he felt alone and in total darkness; the God he had believed in was absent. And most of us can identify with Job's feelings at some point in our lives.

Then I read Isaiah chapter 53 which reveals another face of God:

It was the will of the Lord that his servant should grow like a plant taking root in dry ground. He had no dignity or beauty to make us take note of him. We despised him and rejected him; he endured suffering and pain. No one would even look at him – we ignored him as if he were nothing. But he endured the suffering that should have been ours, the pain that we should have born. He was arrested and sentenced and led off to die, and no one cared about his fate.

In these poetic words, we are confronted with a God who is not removed or distant from our human condition, but suffers, endures and is abandoned along with us. This is not a description of a God who pulls a few strings and a hurricane happens here and an earthquake there. Quite the opposite. The prophet in this passage writes about a God who silently walks in solidarity with us in our pain: who is himself bruised and wounded; who understands our sorrows much more than we understand them ourselves. A God who weeps amidst the debris caused by Turkey's latest earthquake.

This God got involved with our human condition by placing Jesus in our midst. As John's Gospel reminds us, the eternal Word took on 'human flesh' – in other words, experienced human pain and joy. Theologians and church leaders argued among each other for centuries as to whether or not this Jesus was in fact 'fully human'. It is precisely because he is that, 'one of us', that I believe that even in their hellish situation, the folk of western Turkey and of all earth's ravaged places do not walk alone.

The late Cardinal Basil Hume usually replied, when asked to comment on some catastrophe, natural or human, that he had no explanation to offer, only compassion; a quiet sharing accompanied by a respectful silence. And maybe in that silence, we hear the tears of God; a crucified God.

Suffering

Lord,
you who knew suffering,
may I be still for a moment
and remember
all who today are
silenced
violated
imprisoned
cheated
abused
driven from home
exploited
held hostage
robbed
tortured
rejected
betrayed
marginalized
tyrannized
detained without trial
despised
persecuted
abandoned
killed.

29

Dying

Death is not the enemy;
living in constant fear of it is.

Norman Cousins[1]

In the whole expanse of human history there is only one point of contact with the Lord of history: the present moment.

Michel Quoist[2]

May he support us all day long, till the shades lengthen and the evening comes, and the busy world is hushed, and the fever of life is over, and our work is done. Then in his mercy may he give us a safe lodging, and a holy rest, and peace at the last.

John Henry Newman

The late Donald Nicholl is one of my heroes. Donald was a highly respected author, academic and active worker for justice and peace. He wrote widely in the fields of theology, politics and church history. In the 1980s, he was Rector of the famous Ecumenical Institute for Theological Research at Tantur which is situated between Jerusalem and Bethlehem. It was the most significant post he had ever held and his humility and wise guidance touched the lives of literally thousands of visitors to Israel and Palestine. A friend wrote this of Donald's years at Tantur: 'Here, the pastoral, the spiritual and the theological were able to come together to furnish a ministry at once religiously profound and humanly reconciliatory.'

In the early days of May 1997, Donald died, at home, from cancer. Through many years he had faithfully kept a journal, and one of his last entries – written on the 20th March of that year – is not only inspirational but illumines for all of us another spiritual threshold. When he wrote these words, Donald knew that he had a very short time to live. As it turned out, he had just a few weeks. His words point beyond all his physical limitations: they are words of a courageous spirit, reminding us that at the hour of death, despite all our familiar landmarks being rearranged, God's guiding light can be palpably present.

At this stage, there are no outside sources (books, broadcasts etc.) which can help me, unless they evoke my own inner experience over the last 70 years. It is that experience, my guides over these years who have proved faithful, who can help me – the clouds of witnesses who have lived by the Spirit, my ancestors, friends and teachers. They have so much still to tell me, and so I listen to them. And I owe them so much that my thoughts of them become prayers for them and expressions of gratitude ('The very thoughts of a serene person are themselves prayers'). For them, as for me in these straits, Jesus is our lookout and the Holy Spirit is our helmswoman/man. It is to them that I have to listen, to pay attention. Otherwise I shall get diverted and go off course.[3]

Facing death is going to be for all of us an enormously lonely experience, as Donald found when confronting his own terminal illness. Yet, as he says, 'we are surrounded' and also 'held' within a much wider frame of meaning and certainty. Nowadays, we use the phrase 'cloud of witnesses' only in liturgical contexts, but it still carries within it a great truth about our human condition. It focuses our attention on this large group of people through the centuries who have themselves experienced what it means to walk on the spiritual path and who have come to know the companionship of God.

In another entry in his journal (29 March), Donald wrote: 'what happens to me is not my business; it is God's. Mine is to respond to what happens with as much grace as I can muster. My response has to be inspired by the example of Jesus through the Holy Spirit.'

In all of his bodily weakness, he was still able to respond with that grace which had infused his life before illness arrived. And in my own ministry, I have been with many, like Donald, who have been able to 'hand their lives over to God' in a quite remarkable way. In the face of death, they seem to acquire new strengths and fresh insights about the essential purpose of life. They retain all of their rich humanity, even when their frail bodies cry out in pain, while at the same time abandoning themselves utterly to God.

Each year in Westminster Abbey there is a Commonwealth Day Observance Service. At one of these services, this prayer was offered and its words underline something of what Donald Nicholl believed as his own journey on earth neared its completion.

> Hear again my Word Supreme,
> the deepest secret of silence.

Dying

Because I love thee well,
I will speak words of salvation.
Give thy mind to me,
and give me thy heart and thy sacrifice,
and thy adoration.
This is my word of promise,
thou shalt in truth come to me,
for thou art dear to me.
Leave all things behind,
and come to me for thy salvation.
I will make thee free from bondage of pains.
Fear no more.[4]

30

Grieving

Unless thou lead me, Lord,
the road I journey is all too hard.
Through trust in thee alone
can I go on.

Toyohiko Kagawa

Dear Master, may thy light shine
on me now, as it once shone on the shepherds
as they kept their flocks by night.

Oszaki, a leprosy patient

During my time as Warden of Iona Abbey, I made friends with many of the local families on the island. They are friendships I value very highly and I was utterly devastated when I heard that four young people in the village had been drowned while returning from the neighbouring island of Mull. There was one survivor.

The accident happened on a winter evening shortly before Christmas 1998, as the five friends were sailing across the Sound of Iona on their way home. It was a journey each of them had made hundreds of times, in all kinds of weather. All those who died had committed themselves to work on Iona, and their loss to a small, rather remote, rural community is immense. The island has lost a generation of its young folk.

Grieving

A few hours after the tragedy, the body of Robert was washed ashore. The other three, Logie, Davy and Ally, were all found some weeks later not far from the place where their boat had gone down. I was asked by Robert's family to officiate at his funeral service which was held in the Abbey. It was a humbling experience, and brought home to me the courage of all the families in the face of tragedy. As we gathered, in huge numbers, to give thanks to God for Robert's life, I tried to express something of the community's grief in these words:

The other day, a friend on the island said to me, 'For everyone on Iona, these days are a time outside time.' I am certain we all know what she meant. These days on the island, close to Christmas, seem unreal. Days pass by, but the markers of our ordinary lives are far away, particularly as we still await news of our three other friends. Our emotions and spirits are either at a standstill, or in such turmoil we cannot grasp what has taken place.

Yet could it be otherwise at such a time, as a small village comes to terms with the loss of four of its sons? As individuals and as a community we are broken by the sheer scale of events, while at the same time giving thanks to God that one of the five friends has survived to recount the harrowing tale.

As we stand in solidarity with those whose loss is great, hundreds of questions arise in our minds. Why did it happen? Why did four young people who were central to the life of the island have to be taken from us suddenly? Can we be angry with God as we encounter such apparent injustice? Where was God on that winter evening when our boys went down? And what of the future of our community, now filled with many uncertainties? Will the pain ever go away?

Truly, this is a 'time outside time'. We gaze through a mist and all the old certainties seem to have disappeared. For generations to come, the events of that night will be retold many times. We are living through an accidental drowning which has not only shattered our island community but which has evoked a response from people around the world. Today, a vast number of people who feel that Iona is their spiritual home, stand with us in our dark hour.

In a few moments we shall lay Robert to rest in a grave-yard which over the centuries has welcomed crofters and kings. In his burial, we are again reminded of these ancient traditions in our island story. Yet while we may not know much of the kings who lie buried here, we do know of Robert's smiling face, warm heart and zest for life. May he rest with them, in peace.

There is a sentence in the Gospels which says: 'Blessed are the ones who deeply mourn, God's comfort in their hearts is known.' These words announce themselves again to us – reassuring us that whatever may come to us in life, we are held in God's hands. A holding which will not desert us in the face of death, however copious our tears. St Paul put it another way: 'Nothing in heaven or earth can separate us from the love of God through Jesus Christ our Lord.'

In these last days as we talked together, all over the island, one thing became clear. Even in the midst of this present tragedy, we have to rediscover and hold on to the possibilities of new hope which God constantly offers. The four young folk who have died were committed to the island's future welfare. Let us recommit ourselves to many of these things they held dear. And let us, through our tears, be able to celebrate their energy, laughter and wisdom.

That does not imply that there are easy words of comfort or cheap solutions to the incredible pain in our hearts. We are in darkness – but a place such as this Abbey is here to remind us that we do not walk alone. Never. God understands the depth of our pain, which is one reason why we may, in some extraordinary way, feel close to Him, even in our brokenness.

There is a prayer which is rooted in our Celtic inheritance. Its words have comforted literally tens of thousands of women, children and men who have come as pilgrims to this famous place. Today this prayer is not just for these far-away pilgrims, but for us as villagers in the midst of all our uncertainties, tears and countless questions. May it bring a measure of healing and peace; a stillness to our anxious hearts.

> Deep peace of the running wave to you;
> Deep peace of the flowing air to you;
> Deep peace of the quiet earth to you;
> Deep peace of the shining stars to you;
> Deep peace of the Son of Peace to you.

31

Yearning for justice

All the broken hearts
shall rejoice;
all those who are heavy laden,
whose eyes are tired
and who do not see,
shall be lifted up
to meet with
the Motherly Healer.
The battered souls and bodies
shall be healed;
the hungry shall be fed;
the imprisoned shall be free;
all earthly children shall regain joy
in the reign
of the just and loving one
coming for you
coming for me
in this time
in this world.

Asian Woman's Theological Journal

This prophecy of an anonymous Asian woman who has
herself been the victim of exploitation reminds us that the
God of the Bible is a God who longs to bring justice to the

earth. The theme of God's justice echoes through the Bible. The prophet Amos for example, holds out this powerful vision of justice:

> The LORD says: 'I hate your religious festivals; I cannot stand them! When you bring me burnt-offerings and grain-offerings, I will not accept them; I will not accept the animals you have fattened to bring me as offerings. Stop your noisy songs; I do not want to listen to your harps. Instead let justice flow like a stream, and righteousness like a river that never goes dry.'
>
> *Amos 5:21–24*

Hebrew law, based solely on God, is not the expression of the will of the people nor the ruler; and it equates the service to this living God with the service of others. In other words, the duties which the Israelites owed to their God were not confined to the religious realm, but were equally tied in to moral and social life. It was not possible to worship God without having a respect for the rights and dignities of one's neighbour.

Israel rejected the class legislation which was in force at that time in Babylon. Under the law of Moses, justice was the same for all. Biblical legislation was designed to help especially those who were in danger of being the victims of injustice – people such as widows, orphans and foreigners. This fact is underlined by the writer in the book of Deuteronomy: 'Do not cheat a poor and needy hired servant, whether he is a fellow Israelite or a foreigner living in one of your towns. Each day before sunset pay him for that day's work; he needs the money and has counted on getting it. If you do not pay him, he will cry out against you to the Lord, and you will be guilty of sin' (Deuteronomy 24:14–15).

For the people of Israel this overarching vision of justice flowing through society was earthed in an understanding of faith that could not imagine any disconnection between the private and public faces of religious experience. Like the rest of us, the Israelites were a flawed community, but God never let them loose sight of this central plank in the law of Moses. To fail to act justly was a sinful act – an act which brought the judgement of God into play.

Here are words from Leviticus. As I read them I am reminded of the worldwide work of Amnesty International in our own time, as it fights for human rights. They are words which belong to a totally different age from ours, but centuries after their first appearance we cannot escape their central thrust:

> Be honest and just when you make decisions in legal cases; do not show favouritism to the poor or fear the rich. Do not spread lies about anyone, and when someone is on trial for their life, speak out if your testimony can help.

> *Leviticus 19:15–16*

This kind of justice cannot be envisaged apart from an ever-active God who is its ultimate creator and sustainer. The pages of the Old Testament bear witness to a God who is not a passive divinity in a remote heaven, but the opposite. Revealed for humankind in these pages is a God who creates and guides, who intervenes in human history and who stands alongside the afflicted, and from whose heart both justice and righteousness flow in a never-ending stream.

And as a Jew steeped in the Law of Moses, Jesus when visiting the synagogue read one of the great passages concerning God's justice, written by the prophet Isaiah:

Then Jesus went up to Nazareth, where he had been brought up, and on the Sabbath he went as usual to the synagogue. He stood up to read the Scriptures and was handed the book of the prophet Isaiah. He unrolled the scroll and found the place where it is written,

> The Spirit of the LORD is upon me,
> because he has chosen me to bring
>   good news to the poor.
> He has sent me to proclaim liberty to the captives
>   and recovery of sight to the blind;
> to set free the oppressed
>   and announce that the time has come
>   when the LORD will save his people.

Jesus rolled up the scroll, gave it back to the attendant and sat down. All the people in the synagogue had their eyes fixed on him, as he said to them, 'This passage of scripture has come true today as you heard it being read.'

Luke 4:16–21

In a quite specific way, Jesus incarnated God's justice. Through his very being, justice flowed. His message and his life interconnected, and as a prophetic creed which was written in South Africa reminds us: 'In Christ, violence and hatred shall not have the last word; war and destruction have not come to stay for ever.' With his every breath, Jesus witnessed against any expressions of inhumanity. Discrimination, hunger, poverty and all the countless forms of exploitation had, in him, met their ultimate judgement.

And those who claim to be followers of Christ in the modern world in which injustice is rampant, have their work cut out. Or to put it another way – can there be an authentic Christian spirituality which does not have at its heart this yearning and longing for justice within the human family? If we worship a God who shares human-kind's crushing sorrows (as, I believe, God does) can we somehow cut our own life off from these same cries?

In recent years I have been influenced by the life of Oscar Romero who was a bishop in El Salvador. For many years he worked as a church leader, but in a rather conservative, traditional way. Eventually, the agonies of the margina-lized around him reached not only his ears but his heart, and he underwent a radical shift in his spiritual journey. He woke up to a simple fact: that he had, as a pastor, to fight with his people for justice. And because of that identifica-tion, he was eventually killed by the Government of the day.

I believe that what Bishop Romero had learned was the biblical truth that the yearning for justice on earth is God's yearning. As he listened to the agony of his people, he heard the voice of God. There was no alternative but to respond, taking the hard road of solidarity. Underlying this sacrificial commitment was the recognition that conver-sion to Christ had both personal and social imperatives. That the very structures of society, insofar as they have injustice built into them, are concrete forms of sin. They are consequences of human failures throughout history, as well as the continuing stimulus and spur for further sin.

The late Pedro Arrupe, who was a former Superior General of the Jesuits, wrote: 'Our new vision of justice must give rise to a new kind of spirituality, or rather, an expansion of traditional spirituality to include not only the personal but the social. In short, interior conversion is not enough. God's grace calls us not only to win back our whole selves for God, but to win back our whole world for God. We cannot separate personal conversion from structural social reform.'

Sierra Leone in west Africa is a beautiful land which in recent years has known every kind of human agony. Wracked by civil war, dislocated communities, often grieving the murders of their loved ones, wander its dusty roads in search of food and shelter. Some time ago, I had the privilege of being in a refugee camp in the eastern part of the country. In that poverty-stricken place, I felt at home, not least because of the warmth of the welcome. Around me were families bereft of everything, except their innate dignity. Their stories spoke of their courage in the face of a living hell. One afternoon in the camp, I wrote a kind of psalm:

> God who dwells in refugee camps
> and protects the tortured
> will give the homeless
> shelter, and will set
> the exploited free.

> He will lead his people
> across the deserts of
> violence, oppression and fear
> and let justice flourish
> in a wounded land.

> He will weep with them
> day after day
> and will replace the tears
> with songs.

> One day their mourning will end
> and in his strength
> they shall return home
> in peace.

Places like the refugee camp in Sierra Leone forcibly bring home to me that a spirituality which is threaded through with a yearning for justice becomes impoverished without a real love for humanity at its heart. Christ not only saw injustice but made folk on the margins his sisters and brothers. He loved them, and they loved him in return. And he went so far as reminding his listeners that their attitude in terms of compassion and respect towards the oppressed would determine whether or not they would enter the Kingdom of God.

A contemporary psalm from southern Africa tells us that those who weep in their work for justice will come back singing with joy. I know that to be true. As we look around the world, we see all kinds of women and men who are totally immersed in the daily fight for justice and who carry in their lives not anger or bitterness, but tenderness, warmth, laughter and love.

> When the day comes on which our victory
>   will shine like a torch in the night,
>   it will be like a dream.
> We will laugh and sing for joy.
> Then the other nations will say about us,
>   'The Lord did great things for them.'
> Indeed, he is doing great things for us;
> that is why we are happy in our suffering.

Lord, break the chains of humiliation and death,
   just as on that glorious morning
   when you were raised.
Let those who weep as they sow the seeds of justice and
    freedom gather the harvest of peace and reconcilia-
    tion.

Those who weep as they go out as instruments of your
    love
   will come back singing with joy,
   as they will witness the disappearance of hate
and the manifestation of your love in your world.

Psalm 126: Zephania Kameeta[1]

32

Connections

There had not been a drop of water in our part of South India for several weeks. One day, in a crowded bus on my way back from visiting some drought-stricken villages, I wrote these lines:

Lord, I am so comfortable,
the water is running out of our tap
and so near us, just a short bus journey away
there are thousands of families
who don't even have a single drop.

When will the rains come?

Lord, try to open my eyes
to these basic needs of my brothers and sisters.
Keep me from being complacent:
let me not just turn on our tap
and forget their desperate need.

When will the rains come?

Lord, you do not see us as rich and poor,
but as one family,
involved with one another,

bearing each other's burdens,
going the extra mile,
being concerned.

When will the rains come?

I don't know when they will come,
nor do the villagers;
but I do know that I could care more,
and maybe that
by caring more,
my brothers and sisters
will find new strength
even when the wells are dry.

33

Accounting for the use
of our money

Contemplation is not a state of paralysis but of radical self-giving. In the final analysis, to believe in God means to live our life as a gift from God and to look on everything that happens in it as a manifestation of this gift.

Gustavo Gutierrez, contemporary prophet and theologian

It was early summer. The beautifully restored Chapter House within Iona Abbey was crowded with people from various countries. The group was engaged in a wide-ranging discussion about the effects of materialism on our lives. Then came the question. 'Are you really saying that members of the Iona Community have to account for the use of their money?' I replied quite simply: 'Yes, we do.'

The general discussion went up several gears! No longer were we reflecting on 'money' and material things in the abstract, we were moving into the area of 'accountability' which is a word which arouses passionate feeling. George MacLeod, the founder of the modern Iona Community, discovered that response sixty years ago when he insisted that Christians begin to look seriously at what they do with their own money. It was the kind of challenge which did not sit easily in Presbyterian circles in Scotland where the whole issue of money, like sex and politics, was considered taboo. Money is thought of as a purely private matter – surely Jesus never expected us to tell other people what we do with our bank accounts!

'Sharing and accounting for the use of money' is the second discipline to which members of the Iona Community are committed (the first concerns daily Bible reading and prayer). Members are asked, first, to account to each other for the use of their net income – that is gross income less income tax and other statutory contributions. They are then asked to agree on their individual base-line commitments and special circumstances and expenses, thus arriving at a personal disposable income figure from which a tithe (10%) can be deducted.

Within the Iona Community, there are huge differences in the financial positions of members and making these calculations in relation to accountability is far from easy. It would be wide of the mark to suggest that, even where such accountability exists, it happens in a straightforward way. This second discipline of the Community is threaded through from start to finish with problems, questions and much debate among members!

But – and here the 'but' is important – a mechanism for accounting for our money, however flawed, is in place. Money in the Iona Community, is seen as a gift from God and not merely as a personal issue. What we do with it is not just between ourselves and God, but has immense social implications. We live in an inter-connected world and the Community believes that the necessity to account for the use of our money is a fundamental part of any integrated spirituality. That is, a spirituality which seeks to remain true to Christ's teaching in the discovery and making of community in a world divided and permeated with economic injustice.

Money determines so much of our behaviour and at the present time in western societies it is counter-cultural to believe that we have to account for it. 'It is "ours" and we have worked hard for it' is a typical response. Yet as we seek a spiritual path for our lives, should we get quite so irritated when it is suggested that perhaps we have to account for the way we use our money? In this issue of money, where does God come in? Or rather, what is the relationship between our searching for God's light and energy and the way we use our money?

These are hard questions, and it is easier to run from them than to face them, or to feel that accounting for the use of our money is only for members of religious communities who like that kind of thing. Perhaps a helpful way into this challenging area of Christian discipleship is to work with the conviction that we are basically 'stewards' of all we have – our time, our individual abilities and our possessions; to recognize that everything is freely given from the Creator's hand and that in accounting for our money we express a small but significant movement of gratitude to the One who holds all things.

At a personal level, I do not find this kind of accountability something that comes easily. As with most people, it is a hard exercise because the issues around our money are complex and intertwined. What I feel I may need as a 'basic minimum' for daily living appears like a lottery win to my sister or brother in West Africa. Or even the basic provision for my kids may seem like a fortune to a family round the corner. Yet I also accept that this vision of accountability, however poorly handled, enlarges and energizes my spirituality; my journey into God and into establishing a social holiness.

When that visitor on Iona asked if we, as members of the Community, had to actually account for the use of our money, I understood the element of total surprise in her voice. 'Accountability' is a surprising thing if we look at it only as an intellectual or academic exercise. If it becomes that, it loses its essential purpose. Accounting for our money only makes sense when we encounter Christ whose energies of love permeate every facet of our human pilgrimage. And even in my moments of greatest doubt, that is a Christ I long to meet.

> Christ of the market place,
> even when I handle it poorly,
> give me the courage
> to account for my money
> to others,
> and in so doing,
> to recognize again
> that everything in my life
> is a gift
> of your love.

34

Awakening to human rights

We pray for those who have been exiled from their native land, refugees, who have been forced to leave behind their heritage and possessions, their families, and their friends, and those who have had to begin life anew in a foreign culture and among strangers.

Lord, let justice run down like rivers.

We pray for those who are discriminated against on grounds of their race or sex, who offer the gifts of their presence, culture and personality, but find them despised or rejected.

Lord, let justice run down like rivers.

We pray for those who at this moment are being tortured in their bodies or in their minds because of the convictions they hold so dear, that their pain may be eased and that the peace of God may bring them release even in the midst of their suffering.

Lord, let justice run down like rivers.

We pray for all rulers, and those who hold positions of authority in the state and in all the powerful institutions of our society that they may use their power for good and not for evil, that the rights of men and women may no longer be abused.

Awakening to human rights

Lord, let justice run down like rivers.

We pray for all whose basic needs for food, shelter, clothing and healing are not met. Stir up the consciences of peoples and governments, to re-arrange the world's unjust systems; teach us all to live more simply, that others may simply live.

Lord, let justice run down like rivers.

We pray for the nations of the earth that you in your mercy will save them from their folly and humankind from its sin, that people will be set free from vindictiveness and fear, that forgiveness will replace revenge, that none should be in bondage to another, and none shall hold another country in contempt, and you alone will be worshipped all over the earth.

Lord, let justice run down like rivers.

Amnesty International

35

Facing up to racism

Long before the influential MacPherson Report of 1999 spoke of 'institutional racism' within British society, Stanley Hope from Rochdale was prophetically writing in a similar vein. Over a number of years, Stanley has worked tirelessly to alert us all to the destructive effects of entrenched racial attitudes in our communities at large.

His passionate, precise words spring from a life-long involvement with black and Asian families in Britain, and from seeing first-hand the influence of present immigration laws which, he believes, serve to portray members of ethnic minorities as a constant 'threat' to the country. I know from visiting his area how much Stanley's work is valued in the local communities; his is no distant academic voice. He is a quiet prophet; a humble man of faith whose way is one of dialogue and trust. These reflections come from a regular column entitled 'Light a candle, don't just curse the dark!' which Stanley writes in *Coracle*, the bi-monthly magazine of the Iona Community.

The day after the memorial to Stephen Lawrence was splattered with white paint *The Guardian* carried a cartoon by Steve Bell. It showed a Union Jack with a large blob of white paint in the centre. This said it all; that the murder of Stephen Lawrence was a matter of disgrace for the whole country.

Facing up to racism

The Inquiry by Sir William MacPherson says there is institutional racism in the Metropolitan Police. Some weeks ago the Chief Constable of Greater Manchester made a similar admission. But it is not enough simply to charge the police with institutional racism. We must ask how this came about? What helped to create this worst type of racism in the police? And why was it all taken for granted that things had to be like this? Institutional racism is not about personal prejudice, insult or hostility between individuals. It is more about the way things are in a society. It is the daily experience of black and Asian people in Britain; their status, employment prospects, poor housing, poverty, violence, harassment, isolation, exclusion and the network of surveillance which intrudes into their lives. Above all there is the powerful influence of our immigration laws which have served to portray these people as a threat to Britain. For most white people much of this is unknown. For most black and Asian people it has become a way of life. All these together amount to an attack on the worth and dignity of people and communities.

So if it is the institutional racism in the police that worries us, our search must go beyond the police. There is far more that ought to be uncovered that will, to some extent, explain police behaviour.

Foremost amongst what has still to be uncovered and explained to the public is the role of all UK governments since 1962. All of us, police, public and all our institutions, have been deeply influenced by nationality and immigration legislation and the way it has been presented by governments.[1]

For many years, the combined influence of governments,

the law and the power of the media have shaped our response to this issue of racism. As various commentators have pointed out, the person who killed the young black man, Stephen Lawrence, was a child of a culture in which institutional racism has flourished. All of us are in some way responsible for Stephen's brutal killing. We need healing, and the government must revisit and rework the present British Nationality Act which is in itself an expression of discriminatory legislation, bringing pain to countless families and individuals.

The Prime Minister has said that we must confront honestly the racism in ourselves if we are to create a truly multi-ethnic society, finding the will to overcome our ingrained attitudes. John Austin Baker, a former Bishop of Salisbury wrote: 'We simply shall never be able to exert real force and influence against the evils of racism so long as our total cultural, social and political vision is that of a civilisation in which racism is endemic.'

One of the hopeful results of the MacPherson Report, which studied various aspects of racism, is that questions are now being raised where formerly there was only silence. It may be disturbing to examine the old inherited traditions of freedom, equality and protection under the law, democracy and the accountability of those in power, but can we move into a more accepting, tolerant society without such a sustained debate? A debate in which church voices are a part.

Stanley, and other prophets, ask of us difficult questions. That is what makes them prophets, as we see clearly from the Old Testament. How much have we learned from our history about the perspective of those who suffer discrimination because of race or colour and are marginalized in society? Have our traditions of freedom and democracy prevented us from behaving with indifference, even brutality, towards non-white people? How can we reach out in meaningful dialogue and friendship to the 'stranger' in our midst? How do we begin to change our own thinking in such a way that we can value and cherish different cultural traditions?

These are enormously difficult questions, and they are also profoundly spiritual ones. We are all products of our culture and carry a range of hidden assumptions. Yet conversion is possible. With God's help, we can begin to look at our society through a different lens. To awaken to the miracle which is the rich diversity in cultures; to walk as a friend with a person whose skin colour is different from our own; to recognize that we have much to learn from our black and Asian neighbours.

In the Gospel of John, we read of a meeting between Jesus, a Jew, and a Samaritan woman at Jacob's Well. There had been centuries of feuding between the Jews and the Samaritans, and the woman was astonished when Jesus spoke to her and asked if she could draw some water from the well for him. Not only was she a Samaritan, she was also a woman, and for a rabbi to be seen speaking to a woman in public was the end of his reputation. By engaging in conversation with her, Jesus, at a stroke, broke down these various barriers of nationality and orthodox Jewish custom. He cut through entrenched attitudes and in doing so revealed a totally new way of understanding 'the other'. A way which the nations thirst for in our time.

Across the barriers that divide race from race:
Across the barriers that divide the rich from the poor:
Across the barriers that divide people of different faiths:
Reconcile us, O Christ, by your cross.[2]

36

Learning from the
wounds of violence

A friend in Chicago, where I was living at the time, introduced me to Michael Lapsley, an Anglican priest from South Africa. Michael, who had immersed himself in the struggles against apartheid, was forced to live in exile for some years prior to the emergence of the new South Africa.

On 28 April 1990, in Harare, just three months after the release of Nelson Mandela, when it looked as if many of the exiles could return to help in the building of a reinvigorated nation, Michael had an intimate personal experience of violence. One morning when he was opening his mail, a letter bomb, hidden in the pages of two religious magazines, and intended to kill him outright, exploded.

In that terrible moment, he did not lose consciousness or go into shock (for reasons his doctors did not understand) but felt the indescribable pain which accompanied the bombing. Yet even in that dark moment in his life, he was able to recall the presence of God – having a sense that somehow God was being crucified with him in the process of being torn apart. It was a watershed in his life.

In an interview some years later with Radio South Africa, Michael spoke of his inner journey since the day of the bombing.

I had often thought that in the process of struggling against apartheid, that maybe I will die, as I had seen many friends dying in the process. But I had never confronted the possibility that I might suffer permanent major disability. I certainly never conceived that I would lose, as I have, both hands and an eye and I had never met someone who had lost both hands. So even when I experienced this incredible loss I could not imagine what life was going to be like.

Soon after he received these appalling injuries, Michael realised that his main struggle now was to get well, to live life as normally as possible and as joyfully. If he could do that, it would be a victory – especially if he could move on without being filled with bitterness, hatred, self-pity and a desire for revenge.

With the help of God and the support of friends, he has slowly discovered a well of inner healing. Every part of his life is affected by the fact that he has no hands, but he feels that he is probably a much more effective priest with this loss. Now he finds it much easier to identify with the suffering and sacrifice of others, and, because of this, he has grown immeasurably in his spiritual awareness.

Michael now works in South Africa with others who have experienced violence in their lives. His own journey is often painful and extremely difficult, yet he has learned a huge amount about the meaning of forgiveness. About how God can plant in our hearts the ability to forgive even those who have wounded us inwardly and outwardly. He believes that as we discover these dimensions of forgiveness in ourselves, we cease to be prisoners of our circumstances, and can view life through a different lens.

And these inner changes are related to another aspect of

God's healing in us: the healing of the memories. To be able in time to revisit our past, however traumatic it may have been, with a certain degree of inner serenity. In South Africa and other places, this healing of memories is taking place both at a personal and communal level. It is a long process which begins with the telling and re-telling of our stories, perhaps especially those which have been threaded through with violent trauma.

As I listen to people like Michael, I realize that they have much to teach us, even if we have never been part of a struggle like that of South Africa. Violence is everywhere. In our own communities, it is often hidden behind the lace curtains and the tidy gardens, as many recent statistics relating to domestic violence indicate. We will never know the levels of human suffering, even on our own street. The wounds of violence thread through our human journeys, giving birth to limitless pain.

Yet when I met him, I felt that I was with an individual who had not only tremendous physical courage, but who also showed me clearly the necessity to discover Christ's healing touch, whatever the level of our own wounds. Not to keep running away from our multiple outer and inner wounds but rather to be able to allow God to reveal to us how much we are sometimes imprisoned by them. We may have two hands, but we are disabled by violence in other ways, and it is these hurts which we can, as we say in India, lay at the feet of Christ.

> On a summer afternoon
> I met Michael
> who has suffered
> incredible personal violence
> because of his commitment to justice.

His hands were blown away
along with an eye,
by a letter bomb.
A cold, calculated
attempt to
destroy his life
in an instant.

And yet I
see a man
who celebrates life
and lives it to the full,
despite his wounds.

I witness God's healing
through him.
That ability to release
anger and hatred,
and to
be able to forgive
even our enemies.

I've still two hands,
but many wounds inside.
I've still two eyes,
but also inner anger.

Falteringly, I reach out
for Your liberating touch
which has made
Michael
such a whole
person.

37

Hiroshima

A meditation on the Feast of the Transfiguration, 6th of August, and on the events in Hiroshima, Japan on that same day in 1945.

Our kids are asleep
dreaming of fun
like so many others.

It was the same in Hiroshima
many years ago
on August 5th;
kids asleep
dreaming of fun.

And the bomb fell
and they were gone,
turned to ash
with not even
their shadow
remaining on the street.

Transfiguration,
defining new brutalities
beyond imagining.

Hiroshima

Our kids are asleep
dreaming of fun,
and tomorrow on
the Feast of the Transfiguration
we remember that day
when his disciples
saw the face of Jesus
shining like the sun.
And when morning comes
which transfiguration
do we tell the kids about?

Tomorrow is August 6th
and as the world's children dream
their elders
build new bombs
for ten thousand Hiroshimas.

And with the breaking of the dawn
we hear the tears of Christ.

38

Remembering

Suffering God,
sharpen our memories,
teach us to name what is evil
and refuse it,
even when it seems normal or necessary.[1]

Even within the last few years, countless women, children
and men have been killed because of their faith in Christ. It
is easy to forget such a reality amidst the preoccupations of
a 'comfortable Christianity'.

These contemporary martyrs are 'ordinary' people who
have lived hidden lives of enormous courage. Their commitment to the gospel has led them to various kinds of
prophetic resistance in their communities. They have
'named evil even when it seemed normal and necessary'. By
their actions our whole human family is enriched.
Hundreds of books could not contain their names. Here
are the names of five women from the Philippines. In one
sense they are 'ordinary' folk, but for us they are 'extraordinary' and their witness to truth and justice in God's name
continues to make us 'uncomfortable' if we only seek a
'safe' form of Christianity. They are truly our sisters.

Lorena Barros, home-maker and social worker in the

inner-city, shot while walking in the street because of her love for justice.

Angelina Sayat, home-maker and community enabler who died while in the custody of the military because of her concern for the poor.

Puri Pedro, home-maker and church worker, brutally tortured and killed for raising her voice on behalf of local farm workers.

Leticia Celestino, home-maker and factory employee, shot in the picket lines while pleading for a just wage for those who worked alongside her in the factory.

Filomena Asuncion, home-maker and church deacon, who was ruthlessly murdered for trying to make local agricultural workers more aware of their basic rights.

> Blessed are those who are persecuted
> because they do what
> God requires;
> the Kingdom of heaven
> belongs
> to them . . .
>
> *Matthew 5:10*

> Who brings about peace
> is called
> the companion of God
> in the work of creation.
>
> *Jewish saying*

39

Reviving radical prophecy

Biblical faith is prophetically relevant to everything that happens in the world.

The Kairos Document, South Africa

In spite of the attempts to terminate us, assimilate us, subjugate us, annihilate us, we are survivors. After 500 years, we are still here.

Van Lynch, an American Indian of the Choctan tribe who teaches learning-disabled young folk

Turn off your TV and think:
the media is carpet-bombing our consciousness.

written during the Gulf War

One of the reasons I became a member of the ecumenical, international Iona Community was because I regarded it as a prophetic movement within the churches. I also believed, and still do, that the Community approaches that interface between the gospel and society with radical insights. And also with a sense of urgency rooted in a vision which sees no disconnection between the 'spiritual' and the 'material'.

Just over forty years ago, George MacLeod, the founder of the modern Iona Community, wrote a seminal book called *Only One Way Left*. It was a prophetic book which has contemporary relevance as we seek to revisit the ancient and noble tradition of radical prophecy. Here MacLeod is speaking about religious experience.

> Religion has become the hobby of a few. A person who likes music goes to the conservatoire. If painting, the individual seeks out an artist's studio. Or if certain psychic elements predominate in one's make-up, that person 'takes up' God. The real trouble is that the Bible is not about that sort of religion at all. In the Bible, God is a total Sovereign not a personal solace. Authentic solace resides in a serious acceptance of His total sovereignty. God is the hub round which the whole wheel of life revolves. If we make of Him a spiritual hobby, we end by creating Him in our own image. God becomes, though we are unconscious of it, our self-appointed guarantor for all our own little 'isms' about nature and nations and race. Even in our secular society, God remains at the hub, and many of our plans become blueprints ground into the dust beneath the ongoing inexorable wheel of truth. For our God is a God on the move.[1]

As I re-read these words I realize that the power behind them is their prophetic nature. Or to put it another way, their prophetic insight is grounded in a prayerful interpretation of scripture. They are words embedded in a biblically-based understanding of life and of the human condition. And in that sense they are also transforming words, illumining certain features of Christ's message for the world. They come from the pen of an individual who passionately believed that this whole world, in all its fragmentation and beauty, is actually held in the hands of a living God.

In recent years, many of the churches, particularly outside the western world, have articulated powerfully this tradition of radical prophecy. Outstanding examples are evident in the various expressions of liberation theology which call into question, in the light of biblical truth, many of society's underlying assumptions, especially about poverty and exploitation. This theology, dealing not only with personal but also structural sin, carries within it a strong prophetic message, not just for those communities in which it finds its birth, such as Latin America, but for all of us.

These voices of radical prophecy challenge any bland interpretation of Scripture. They speak, not of some 'neutral' God, but of One who constantly interacts with people in the struggles of their lives. Zephania Kameeta of Namibia poetically and prophetically writes:

> The church on earth does not walk in silence or neutrality, but she sings with a clear voice the song of victory and liberation. A hymn that shakes the evil powers and pulls down all the destructive schemes and idealogies. A hymn that lifts up the oppressed, poor and despised people from the dust and brings down the mighty from their thrones. A hymn that calls the whole universe to Jesus Christ.[2]

One of my colleagues in the Church of South India once wrote to me in a similar vein, and I have often re-read his letter, particularly when it seems that some of the churches in my own country are concerned only with their own survival. Tragically, some years later, he was killed in a road accident. I still cherish his memory, his friendship and his prophetic wisdom. He taught me so much.

Dear Peter,

Theology for our oppressed women and men in the villages where we both work in this part of South India is not an intellectual exploration. It is a daily struggle to understand the meaning of salvation in Christ from a place of alienation, exploitation and shame. It is a theology which aims at liberation through Christ who walks with the poor himself.

In the continuing struggle we stand with our people.

Your loving friend,

Clement.

In their prophetic vision, George MacLeod, Zephania Kameeta and my friend Clement reach back into that rich heritage of the biblical prophets. As they focused on their own societies in that time, they interpreted the hopes and fears of their peoples in the knowledge that God's wisdom and judgement permeate every facet of human existence. They appeared to have no hesitation in warning God's people of what would happen to them if they neglected their Creator's promise to them. Yet men like Jeremiah, who never minced his words, were also sensitive to the aspirations of ordinary people, believing that they had a special place in the heart of God's purpose.

In many passages, Jeremiah spoke with emotion about the ways in which he had suffered because God had called him to be a prophet. As one commentator said: 'The word of the Lord was like fire in his heart – he could not keep it back.' And it is this sense of urgency earthed in that 'fire in the heart' which for me is an important element in contemporary radical prophecy.

Perhaps I can put it another way. Authentic prophecy from Christians concerning society can only emerge from a profound prayerful awareness of the world, and from walking in solidarity with it. That is why the writings of Archbishop Oscar Romero of El Salvador challenge us all so profoundly. In the later years of his ministry he came to realize that his life had to be identified totally with the often violent and painful struggles of the marginalized. He had not always believed that, but the cries of the dis-possessed in his own country changed the whole direction of his life. As he once wrote: 'I am a shepherd who, with his people, has begun to learn the beautiful and difficult truth; our Christian faith requires that we submerge ourselves in this world.' That submersion in society eventually led to his murder by Salvadorian Government agents as he cele-brated Mass.

Radical prophecy. We need it not only in El Salvador but in every country. A gospel which challenges, unsettles, and which is unafraid to address what Romero called 'the real sins of society'. Few in our time have expressed this need better than Archbishop Romero himself:

> A church that doesn't provoke any crisis, a gospel that doesn't unsettle, a word of God that doesn't get under anyone's skin, a word of God that doesn't touch the real sin of society around it, what gospel is that? Very nice, pious considerations that don't bother anyone; that's the way many would like preaching to be. Yet does such a gospel really love the world we live in? The gospel of Christ is courageous; it is the 'good news' of Him who came to transform and take away the world's sin.[3]

Jock Dalrymple, a Scottish Roman Catholic priest, was like Romero a guide and friend to many. He was also a visionary; perhaps a prophet without honour, although countless folk recognized the prayerful wisdom which gave birth to his spiritual insights. Shortly before his death in the mid-1980s, Jock wrote an article for the *Beda Review*. His words have great relevance for this new century.

I think the change in Christian spirituality is only just beginning to be felt, perhaps it is still a minority viewpoint. The press within the Roman Catholic church is full of powerful resistance to its implications. To be asked to change the habits of a lifetime is never easy for people. We are only just beginning to get away from the idea that holiness consists in prayer and charity and abstention from politics.

My guess is that the next twenty-five years of spiritual progress will see a huge increase in our awareness of fighting for human rights as part of following the Gospel, as the exciting thinking of liberation theology trickles eastwards to Europe.

I am also bound to confess that in moments of gloom I see the opposite taking place, and our spirituality retreating into a self-indulgent, self-nurturing movement which turns its back on the oppressed people of the world, Christ's brothers and sisters.

If that were to happen, it would signal the end of Europe spiritually. You can only go so far in taming the Gospel. If you persist in removing the disturbing elements, you wake up one day to find you have lost the Gospel altogether.[4]

40

Seeking moral imagination

I am sure that God is alive and well in this country, but mercifully not dependent on the churches alone for his effective disclosure.

Elizabeth Templeton

Society is desperate for a conversation about public issues set in a moral framework. I invite you to encourage that conversation, to build a sense of community that flows from your practice and your conviction that Christians and creative ideas are not a contradiction in terms.

Margaret Steinfels, writer

Could it be that our present culture is providing those of us in the churches with a wholesale challenge to reach out for a more mature expression of faith?

Bernard Häring

Moral imagination. Some years ago, the American writer Mary Richards, employed this phrase when talking about the link between meditation and compassion. Mary wrote:

We are not always able to feel the love we would like to feel. But we may behave imaginatively; envisioning and eventually creating what is not yet present. This is what I call 'moral imagination' and there can be no compassion without it. From the child's ability to imagine grows well the adult's capacity for compassion; the ability to picture the sufferings of others, to identify. In one's citizenship or the art of politics, it is part of one's skill to imagine other ways of living than one's own.[1]

Moral imagination comes not just by sitting in an arm chair, but in the process of doing and of making. In this sense, it is an act of creation, rediscovering that biblical injunction which is found in the book of Genesis, that we are all creators made in the one Creator's image and likeness. It means that as human beings we can envisage alternatives; other ways of viewing a situation whether locally or globally. It is an inner power which enables us to imagine with others, and to be changed by this imagining. Its roots are in our listening to God; that movement into the deep, still places of our souls.

Mary Richards testifies to her own growth in compassion as her moral imagination developed. One day on a beach in North Carolina, before any civil rights legislation, she noticed the segregated water fountains but also the white folk trying to get dark in the sun, a sun shining equally on the black and white swimmers. 'My entire feeling about the sun was affected. That's what I mean; you take it all in, the politics and the recreation and the social attitudes, the environment and the water fountains. And you ask, how can we keep our recreation and our politics separate? How can we not see what our eyes behold? As our perceptions become more and more co-ordinated, we grow in justice.'[2]

Throughout the Old Testament we see this kind of moral

imagination in the lives of the prophets. Out of their profound faith in the living God, sprung creative prophecy which, because it saw political and social alternatives, was revolutionary. For them, justice was about doing something – about carving and moulding alternative social and religious structures. Theirs was not a spiritual solitariness, or a mere feeling about what was wrong in society. They lived justice; a justice which flowed from their moral imagination. In this way they were creators of a different human future – envisioning what was not yet a reality for their peoples.

The Old Testament prophets did not only turn inwards to seek peace and calm, for they knew that peace without justice is a lie, a cover-up. They were not introvert meditators in the habit of dwelling only upon their private experiences. Within their lives, this linkage of prayer and compassion which gave birth to their moral imagination always turned them outwards towards society. Their compassion became active as it sought to right injustice, mitigate misery and bring people home to God. In these memorable words of Isaiah, 'God will settle disputes among great nations, they will hammer their swords into ploughs and their spears into pruning-knives' (Isaiah 2:4), we come face to face with a powerful envisioning of a non-violent path for the nation. Here was moral imagination applied to a vast human canvas.

On the front line between Roman Catholic and Protestant areas in Belfast are a couple of small houses which are home to the Cornerstone Community. This Community brings together people from both religious traditions in the work of reconciliation. In their witness I see a creative expression of moral imagination. In their quiet way, the Cornerstone people envisage a quite different future for

Northern Ireland: a future free of bigotry and discrimination. That hope is not just something they speak about, but act out in their lives, often in the face of threat, misunderstanding and criticism. Their prayers married to compassionate insight about the prevailing situation in Northern Ireland have allowed a rich moral imagination to flourish. In that sense they are prophets; humble prophets all too aware of their own limitations.

When I had the privilege of visiting the Cornerstone Community, I was struck by the fact that here was a small group of ordinary folk who had not given in to the idea that the peace process, however tough, was to be abandoned. Rather it was from these interminable discussions and false starts that they knew hope would spring. In living ecumenically they were themselves showing that religious barriers and suspicion could be overcome. They symbolized 'another way'. And when the history of this sad time in their country comes to be written, it will be clear that those with a sustained moral imagination were the peacemakers and bridge-builders.

Another sign of moral imagination at work is seen in the Jubilee 2000 campaign. This movement is calling on governments in various countries to cancel the burden of debt which rests on the shoulders of a billion of the world's poorest people. It is now a worldwide movement on the brink of a historic achievement. Already the leaders of the world's richest nations have agreed to certain debt cancellation, and recently the British Prime Minister said, 'This is an issue whose time has come. I will personally do whatever I can to make it happen.' The campaign has won plaudits from many commentators, and its effectiveness has been acknowledged by governments, the World Bank and by the International Monetary Fund. The situation *vis-à-vis* the burden of debt is changing, as Jubilee 2000 continues its campaigning work and plans to stage many major public events in various countries. Its work has already made millions of people aware of the suffering brought to whole countries because they are unable to repay their international debt.

As I look at the present task facing Jubilee 2000, I think back to the time, only a few years ago, when a comparatively small number of people envisaged a debt-free start for a billion of our sisters and brothers. Without a vital moral imagination expressing itself through their commitment, the global community might still be unaware of this international injustice. Their perceptions of our global situation had become integrated, and the founders of the Campaign acted upon their insights. A new truth was born: that the world community should no longer tolerate the misery which debt brings to millions of families across the globe. And however this campaign moves forward, the human family can never again go back to a time when it is unaware of the plight of the poorest people on earth. Our global awareness has changed for ever.

One of the great spiritual waymarks of our age is this resurgence of moral imagination. A way of perceiving grounded in that marriage of prayer and compassion. Without such imagination we perish, locked into out-dated structures and atrophied behaviour – whether in politics, the churches or in our local neighbourhoods. This creative compassion is always evolving and never static; moral imagination prevents our retreat into boredom and cynicism. It is not too much to believe that in some of the toughest situations in the world today, moral imagination is giving birth not only to healing and reconciliation, but also to a deeper awareness of what it means to be a human

being in a world marked by tremendous uncertainty. A fact
I tried to express in these words:

> Don't hide,
> don't run,
> but rather
> discover in the midst of fragmentation
> a new way forward:
> a different kind of journey
> marked by its fragility,
> uncertainty
> and lack of definition.
> And on that path,
> to hold these hands
> that even in their brokenness
> create a new tomorrow.
> To dance at the margins,
> and to see
> the face of Christ
> where hurt
> is real and
> pain a way of life.
> To be touched
> in the eye of the storm,
> aware that tomorrow
> may not bring peace.
> Impossible, you say;
> let me retreat
> and find my rest.
> What rest, my friend,
> in these fragmented times?

41

Welcoming the provisional

Jesus said to the crowd who followed him, 'this is what I want you to know:

Don't worry about what you are going to eat
    or what clothes you are going to wear;
what you are is more important than what you eat,
    what you are is more important than what you wear.

Look at the wild birds:
    they don't go out farming;
    they have no store-house or barn;
God feeds them.
    How much more than wild birds you mean to God!

Look at the wild flowers:
    they don't work like mothers at home.
Yet believe me, King Solomon wasn't robed as gloriously
  as a wild flower.

God dresses the wild grass –
    blowing in the field today,
    a bonfire on the farm tomorrow.
How much more will God look after you!
You don't trust him enough.'

Matthew 6:25–30[1]

In commenting on this passage, the New Testament scholar

William Barclay made an important point. For him, Jesus was not advocating a thoughtless, improvident attitude to life, but was warning against a care-worn, worried, fearful way of living each day. The Jews were familiar with such teaching. The rabbis taught that one ought to meet life's complexities with a combination of prudence and serenity. But at the same time they said, 'The person who has a loaf in his basket and who says "What shall I eat tomorrow?" has little faith in God.'

In the Gospel, Jesus makes clear that if God has given us the amazing gift of life, surely we can live in a trusting way for lesser things. He reminds his listeners that the wild birds are not constantly anxious about their future, nor do they stock up endless security arrangements, yet they are precious to God. And it is the same with the scarlet poppies and anemones on the hillsides of Palestine. In their brief life they are clothed with a beauty which far surpasses even the luxurious garments of a monarch. Yet within a short time, now withered and dried, they may be used in a clay oven to speed up a local woman's baking or placed on a bonfire in the farmyard.

It is easy to dismiss these poetic words of Christ because they appear to contain only an abstract ideal. We live in the real world: the world of redundancies, cancers, broken relationships and financial hardship. We may be able to believe that the birds and the flowers are taken care of by God, but our concerns demand that we take life seriously and do all we can to make ourselves secure. Even when we are eighteen or nineteen, pension companies are advising us about the size of our pension at sixty-five! Within modern living, there is not too much attention paid to the provisional nature of life. We can't leave things to chance – or to God – that would be all too threatening.

As I reflect on my own spiritual journey, these astonishing words of Jesus here in Matthew's Gospel seem to be more relevant than ever, for they are essentially about an inner attitude of 'trust'. Let me put that another way. Even in the face of our multiple daily concerns and questions, does God really want us to live, day after day, in a state of never-ending worry? Is it not possible to live more serenely – going along with the various flows which touch into our daily experiences; not constantly battling to arrange life on our own terms; accepting and welcoming the fact that circumstances are never static and that, despite all our attempts to 'feel secure', much is provisional.

In welcoming the provisional into our daily living, we are not being reckless or other-worldly. Rather, we are recognising that not everything can be planned; that the next five months or five years may bring many major changes; that surrendering our lives to these inner voices is not necessarily a bad move! Michael Leunig in Australia has written an evocative prayer which draws us into that 'inner truth' whose message frees us to live with a greater acceptance of the provisional.

Dear God,
    We struggle, we grow weary, we grow tired. We are exhausted, we are distressed, we despair. We give up, we fall down, we let go. We cry. We are empty, we grow calm, we are ready. We wait quietly.
    A small, shy truth arrives. Arrives from without and within. Arrives and is born. Simple, steady, clear. Like a mirror, like a bell, like a flame. Like rain in summer. A precious truth arrives and is born within us. Within our emptiness.
    We accept it, we observe it, we absorb it. We

surrender to our bare truth. We are nourished, we are changed. We are blessed. We rise up.

For this we give thanks.

Amen[2]

Surrendering to the bare truth of God within our lives, places in a new perspective many of our worries, fears and hesitations. They don't disappear, but we begin to see them through a different lens, and awake to the reality that movement and change accompany every part of our journey. We begin to walk with another range of securities, and our emptiness is filled. We relax because we know that endless worrying is actually destructive to the task in hand.

In societies which are not cushioned by affluence, people have no alternative but to live provisionally. They are thankful for the gift of life in each new day, despite all the prevailing uncertainties. To say that is not to romanticize poverty and the endless toil which accompanies it, but to suggest that we can learn much from those who will never know the meaning of long-term security. As a prayer from Tahiti puts it:

O Lord, our palm trees can no longer hide us from the world.
Strengthen our hearts that we may look with confidence to the future.

In all of this I am not trying to turn the clock back; we live within late modernity and within its fragmentations and pluralities. Yet that in itself implies living with risk, with uncertainty, with the 'unknown future', with the 'provisional'. So why not welcome that provisionality with open arms, as the Gospel suggests, rather than fighting it at every turn? Why don't we embrace the flowing movements in life with hope rather than fear, trusting that God has not abandoned us? Etty Hillesum in her 'An Interrupted Life' made the case for welcoming the provisional nature of life with clarity. For me, her words resonate with a bare truth deep inside my being as I try to open myself to life's ebbs and flows.

God, take me by your hand, I shall follow you dutifully, and not resist too much. I shall evade none of the tempests life has in store for me, I shall try to face it all as best I can. But now and then grant me a short respite. I shall never again assume, in my innocence, that any peace that comes my way will be eternal. I shall accept all the inevitable tumult and struggle. I delight in warmth and security, but I shall not rebel if I have to suffer cold, should you so decree. I shall follow wherever your hand leads me and shall try not to be afraid.

I shall try to spread some of my warmth, of my genuine love for others, wherever I go. But we shouldn't boast of our love for others. We cannot be sure that it really exists. I don't want to be anything special, I only want to try to be true to that in me which seeks to fulfil its promise. I sometimes imagine that I long for the seclusion of a nunnery. But I know I must seek you amongst people, out in the world.[3]

Do not fear
what may happen tomorrow.
The same loving father
who cares for you today
will care for you tomorrow
and every day.

Welcoming the provisional

Either he will shield you
from suffering,
Or he will give you
unfailing strength to bear it.
Be at peace then,
and put aside all anxious
thoughts and imaginings.

St Francis de Sales

42

Building bridges

I think of places where bridges must be built:
as people hold dialogue with those of other faiths;
among churches of my own locality;
with those who are made to feel they have no place
in society – hard-drug addicts; alcoholics;
those rejected by family or church, or both.

Make me a builder of bridges, Lord:
help me to listen more and talk less;
to learn, rather than to give advice;
to receive, when I would rather give;
to acknowledge that I do not have all the truth;
to be rejected, hurt and humbled
. . . and, ever more deeply, to go on loving.[1]

God our Mother and Father, be with us as we learn
to see one another with new eyes, hear one another with
new hearts, and treat one another in a new way.[2]

In Northern Ireland, all those who are associated with the
ecumenical Corrymeela Community have been seeking to
build bridges and bring healing to ancient divisions. This
work has brought them praise and disapproval, but for
many of us the ministry of reconciliation based at
Corrymeela is a sign of God's presence within a divided

society. Without new bridges being built among people, the pain of misunderstanding will continue, not just in Northern Ireland but across the world.

We have never needed genuine reconciliation more than today. The twentieth century saw more than 100 million women, children and men perish in wars and civil conflict. Alongside these horrors must be placed authoritarian governments which have brutalized their citizens in various ways by imprisonment, torture, genocide, oppression and intimidation. The amount of suffering we humans can inflict upon one another seems limitless.

Part of the process of reconciliation has to do with creating social structures through which a fractured society, such as East Timor or Kosovo, can be reconstructed as truthful and just. The other part is spiritual, and this, as the folk of Corrymeela know well, is no easy task. How is bridge-building experienced? In what ways can this experience become a key to a new way of living, able to be shared in a wider context? In what ways can the message of the gospel lift us from entrenched attitudes and see the other person through new eyes?

Whatever the form reconciliation may take in a specific situation, whether in a family or in a country, it is at its heart the work of God. We read in the Gospels that through the life and ministry of Christ we are brought into the heart of God's love, and that because of that, authentic, long-term reconciliation between one another is not a human achievement alone. As we try to be bridge-builders in our neighbourhoods and family circles, we soon realize that it is God's work; a work demanding prayerful listening to that voice within us all. And when people and countries do become reconciled with one another, we are in the presence of 'a moment of grace', a moment of God's surprising.

If we have experienced the gift of reconciliation within our own family circle, we know that we have become richer human beings because of what has happened. We have incorporated the experience of being reconciled into our personal journey, and our emotional and spiritual understanding has been enlarged. This is not to say that the pain or injustice of the past has been denied or obliterated, but that the memory of it has been reshaped and transformed. Any form of bridge-building among people is not about going back. Rather it is about addressing the past adequately so that we can go forward.

One rather unfashionable quality which bridge-building requires of us is tenderness. That kind of engaged tenderness which arises not from weakness or false piety, but from a humility which is located deep in our humanity. The world is already full of harsh voices which are unwilling to listen to another person, or take on board a new idea, or admit to being wrong. We cry out for tenderness in one another, not for more strident voices which regard any form of dialogue as the work of darkness!

In the 1990s, as the new South Africa emerged, the local Council of Churches initiated many discussions about the real meaning of blacks and whites living together after years of hatred and misunderstanding. The churches knew that bridges had to be built, but saw all too clearly the enormous problems facing a united country. Yet their vision, rooted in an imaginative biblical perspective, is a guide to us all as we attempt the difficult task of building bridges within our often fractured families and divided communities.

We are a people composed of many races, many languages, many religious traditions, many political parties, many cultures. We are poor and rich, women and men, young and old. We have emerged from a history of strife and death to seek a future of life and health. We acknowledge the presence of Christ among us who reconciles the world.

We struggled against each other: now we are reconciled to struggle for one another.
We believed it was right to withstand one another: now we are reconciled to understand one another.
We endured the power of violence: now we are reconciled to the power of tolerance.

We built irreconcilable barriers between us: now we seek to build a society of reconciliation.
We suffered a separateness that did not work: now we are reconciled to make togetherness work.
We believed that we alone held the truth: now we are reconciled in the knowledge that Truth holds us.

We puffed ourselves up to demand others to bow down to us: now we are reconciled to embrace one another in humility before God.
We do not pretend we have already won or are already perfect: now we are reconciled to press on together to the fullness which lies ahead.

We are reconciled to the patience and persistence that makes peace;
to the transparency and fairness that makes justice;
to the forgiveness and restitution that builds harmony;
to the love and reconstruction that banishes poverty and discrimination;

to the experience of knowing one another that makes it possible to enjoy one another;
to the spiritual strength of the one God, who made us of one flesh and blood, and loves us.[3]

43

Giving thanks

God, my Shepherd!
I don't need a thing.
True to your word,
you let me catch my breath
and send me in the right direction.
Your trusty shepherd's crook
makes me feel secure.
You revive my drooping head;
my cup brims with blessing.
Your beauty and love chase after me
every day of my life.
I'm back in the house of God
for the rest of my life.

from a translation of Psalm 23 [1]

One evening in early May as I looked out of my office window in Iona Abbey, a magnificent double rainbow arched across the Sound of Iona and the neighbouring island of Mull. It was spell-binding in its beauty, and I felt in that moment an immense sense of gratitude for everything in God's world – rainbows, dogs, smiles, grannies – you name it! So I wrote this:

Lord of Life,
we celebrate your countless gifts,
in days and nights,
in rainbows and rain,
in touch, dream and smile,
in partners who love,
in kids who cuddle,
in grannies who listen,
in friends who care,
in dogs that lick,
in hands that sew,
in food on the table;
yet above all,
in your coming among us,
walking our roads,
calling our names,
enfolding our lives,
inviting us home.

44

Announcing Good News

These ten commandments are not meant to supersede the traditional Ten Commandments found in the Old Testament! They serve a different purpose, and reflect the plural nature of our times. They challenge us to keep linking our faith with the world, and are grounded in God's ever-renewing activity as both Creator and Sustainer of all that is.

1. You will encounter the God of history
   (celebrating the biblical narrative which calls us to sustained prayer and outreaching love)

2. You will wonder at the breadth of your Creator
   (celebrating the glory and mystery of creation)

3. You will take yourselves seriously as a people of God
   (celebrating the call to discipleship and to active obedience given to every Christian, not just to the ordained!)

4. You will extend your hand to your fellow Christians
   (celebrating the path of unity among the churches)

5. You will acknowledge that I am present among all peoples
(celebrating the diversity of religious traditions)

6. You will allow common sense to prevail
(celebrating that partnership between science and religion)

7. You will take sides with the poor
(celebrating the demands for justice on earth)

8. You will make the earth a paradise
(celebrating our responsibilities to the environment)

9. You will accompany religious nomads
(celebrating the challenges of the secular world)

10. You will swell the ranks of the peacemakers
(celebrating an engaged spirituality)[1]

45

Celebrating

O God, you are my God,
and I long for you.
My whole being desires you;
like a dry, worn-out, and waterless land,
my soul is thirsty for you.
Your constant love
is better than life itself,
and so I will praise you.
I will give thanks
as long as I live;
I will raise my hands to you
in prayer.
My soul will feast and be satisfied,
and I will sing
glad songs of praise to you.
As I lie in bed, I remember you;
all night long, I think of you,
because you have always been my help.
In the shadow of your wings
I sing for joy.
I cling to you,
and your hands keep me safe.

Psalm 63:1–8

This was no ordinary Sunday worship service, a kind of liturgical interruption into the real business of living. This was celebration. Dying they are; in every sense, from individual fatality by bomb, mine or bullet, to the slow asphyxiation of a community. Dying yes, but yet beautifully alive.

Charles Elliot, formerly Director of Christian Aid
during a visit to northern Namibia

It was Harvest Festival. The sun was slowly sinking across the great plains of southern India as we came near the small village – 'cow dust time' – when everything across the land seems still and the great heat of the day has passed. As we entered the village in the gathering darkness, we were greeted by a real sense of celebration. The little church, brightly lit up against the surrounding darkness, was like a bright star in a dark sky. Although the church was lit by a few electric bulbs, it was the rows of candles on all the windows which added to the magic. The flames of these candles were blowing gently in the evening breeze, reminding us of the symbol of light which is both at the heart of the Christian gospel and deep within the ancient spiritual traditions of Hinduism. Everywhere there were children, most of them singing Tamil songs with great enthusiasm. As we approached the church, several of the women welcomed us with a traditional dance. They danced with their whole being, and with deep devotion. And in the simple beauty of their movements, a thousand words were spoken.

The scene inside the church would be hard to describe. Every square inch was taken up with people: old men, young men; old women, young women; youths and children and tiny babies; and any space that was left over was occupied with hens, ducks, a jumping goat, vegetables, fruit, baskets of rice and many other things from the village fields. The whole place seemed to be praising the Creator, not least the large cockerel perched on a bag of paddy and gazing earnestly at a picture of Christ hanging behind the Communion table. Another hen almost caught fire during the second hymn as it squeezed against a candle on the window ledge. Five ducks sat under my stool and just as we began a rather long prayer, one of them jumped over onto the paddy and began to have supper.

As the service went on, the young children began to go to sleep one by one. Soon there were many little figures spread across the floor. Sometimes the mothers and grandmothers dozed lightly with them, but when we sang the familiar Tamil lyrics all were awake and the music could be heard in the surrounding villages. The whole church was alive with music and it drifted out across the moonlit fields, over the tall palm trees and down to the tank where the buffaloes rested.

After the service was over, we shared with a village family in their evening meal. Their small hut was full of warmth, love and welcome. Then we returned to the church where the elders were auctioning the hens, the ducks, the vegetables and the paddy for church funds. There was a great deal of laughter and much noise. It was very late when the auction ended, but by now no-one was tired.

Soon we started on our homeward journey. But we were returning with more than we had come with, for we had purchased some of the ducks at the auction. We said our farewells and headed down the mud road. Above us the stars were shining over the empty fields. Within a few minutes we could no longer hear the singing and the laughter and the shouts of children and the night was still and very silent; a deep stillness. The Harvest Festival was over for another year.

Yet the joy and fellowship of that evening would not be forgotten, for in that poor village we had experienced the riches of Christ.

46

Journeying on with hope and laughter in our hearts . . .

May the raindrops fall lightly on your brow,
May the soft winds freshen your spirit,
May the sunshine brighten your heart,
May the burdens of the day rest lightly upon you,
And may God enfold you in the mantle of his love.

Gaelic blessing

Hope and laughter-filled women, children and men have made these pages live; a rainbow people who know that God is around. People who shine. Some are famous, many are not, but the living Spirit of God is their constant way-mark. All of them know uncertainty and also laughter's healing art. Mother Teresa of Calcutta used to say that God was not on the look-out for 'extraordinary' people, but for ordinary folk with extraordinary love in their hearts. In the course of my wanderings, I have met many like that, and a few of them have appeared in these reflections.

Their journeys have touched into mine, in one way or another, and their lives can inspire us all. Bede and Helen, Charlene and Bill, Emilio and Sue, Rigobertu and Basil, David and Angelina, Sola and Helder, Gustavo and Mary

– and many, many more. And as I think of them, I offer a simple prayer of gratitude for the fact that God put them on earth; what a gift! They are for me, Christ's life-enhancing waymarks, even as some of them cry out from situations of oppression and betrayal.

We are surrounded by such people. In every street, in every neighbourhood, in every town there are shining lives. You yourself may be a 'living waymark' in your community: a bearer of optimism and of compassionate engagement. A person who within your inner journey has touched both the heights and the depths, and because of that is able to reach out to others with tenderness, insight and laughter.

Moving on in hope. Can we do otherwise when we look around at the beauty and the diversity of the natural world? Several of the poems and meditations which I have included in this book have moved me to tears because of their inner wisdom, prayerful awareness and lyrical sensitivity. As we open to creation itself, we constantly catch glimpses of the transcendent, of divine glory silently articulated in the falling leaf or the long-jump of a red squirrel on the pines. For our spiritual and physical survival depends more than ever on our relationship with the wind, the rain, the mountains, the rivers, the woodlands and meadows and all their inhabitants.

And laughter is also one of our companions on this journey; the gift to be able to celebrate life which I saw again and again in some of the poorest homes in India. A laughter which is linked to an inner spiritual freedom, and to an acceptance that most of life is both provisional and risk-filled. As I noted in the dedication of this book, the families in the villages of India taught me much about authentic living; of being present to the moment, acknowledging God's reality at every turn.

Journeying on with hope and laughter in our hearts . . .

One question which I have raised, perhaps indirectly, in these pages, is this. Is it possible to experience deep hope and genuine celebration in our souls without having travelled along that road marked by disappointment, pain and insecurity?

I have often thought about this. Our society goes to great lengths to make individuals feel comfortable, secure and content. We are told by governments, whether of the Left or Right, that we have 'never had it so good'. Even some of the churches are locked into a message which contains only soothing words of comfort. Certainly the gospel narrative brings reassurance, but it also carries another truth. Helder Camara put it succinctly in one of his magnificent prayers:

> Come, Lord, change our lives,
> shatter our complacency.
> Take away the quietness
> of a clear conscience.
> Press us uncomfortably,
> for only thus
> that other peace is made,
> your peace.
>
> *Helder Camara*[1]

As we travel further into this new century, most of us will not be living lives of ease, surrounded by every comfort. Already poverty affects a huge proportion of the world's people; for millions, that means absolute poverty. Economists predict that, unless there are drastic economic changes at a global level, poverty will touch into the lives of more and more families on earth, and not just in certain parts of the world. Where pockets of wealth remain, it will become abundantly clear that unless resources are more equitably shared, the human future itself is in question. Even now, does our Creator want us to rest quietly while so many of our sisters and brothers are without even basic shelter?

I raise this issue not out of pessimism, but because I believe that our prevailing rampant materialism is birthing not only global injustice on a vast scale, but tremendous spiritual impoverishment in our lives. Have we lost the creative and moral imagination to live more simply so that others might simply live?

We belong together; our essential interconnectedness is a fact, and it could become, if we captured the vision, the source of healing as a people, and the root of our hope and laughter. We do not walk alone; never have, and never will do. Of course we are different from one another, hugely different, but it is as we try, however falteringly, to reach out to one another that we awaken to our full humanity. It's about loving God *and* our neighbour; an insight which has been around for a long time!

One last thought. I would not have written this book had I not believed in both hope and laughter (that innate ability to celebrate life) as special gifts of God for our time. There is a lot of cynicism about, and many people feel overwhelmed by the rate of change, and by the sheer precariousness of it all. Yet through the lens of an engaged spirituality we see that God has not abandoned this world, and that the steady light of Christ's healing presence continues to glow, often in very dark situations.

We travel together, not on an unknown path, but on one which is marked at every turn with God's amazing waymarks. As the Gaelic blessing says, the raindrops are falling lightly on our brows, and a mantle of God's love enfolds our continuing journey.

47

Moving on in the light of God

We must close the meeting, my people!

This is merely a resting place, a place of transit,
where humanity and God pause
before taking to the road again.

Go, my people,
you are ready to set sail;
Your country is not here.
You are a wayfaring people,
strangers,
never rooted in one place,
pilgrims moving towards
an abiding city further on.

Go forth, my people,
go and pray further off;
love will be your song
and life your celebration.

Go,
you are the house of God,
stones cut according
to the measure of God's love.

Waymarks

You are awaited, my people,
and I declare to you,
Word of God,
I am going with you.

The United Congregational Church of Southern Africa[1]

48

Experiencing blessing

May the blessing of light be upon you,
light without and light within.
May the blessed sunlight shine upon you and warm
  your heart,
till it glows like a great peat fire,
so the stranger may come and warm himself at it,
and also a friend.
And may the light shine out of the two eyes of you
like a candle set in two windows of a house,
bidding the wanderer to come out of the storm.
And may the blessing of the rain be upon you,
the soft, sweet rain.
May it fall on your spirit,
so that all the little flowers may spring up,
and shed their sweetness on the air.
And may the blessing of the great rains be on you,
may they beat upon your spirit, and wash it fair and
  clean
and leave there many a shining pool where the blue of
  heaven shines,
and sometimes a star.
And may the blessing of the earth be on you,
the great, round earth:
may you ever have a kindly greeting for them you pass

as you go along the roads.
May the earth be soft under you
when you rest out upon it,
tired at the end of the day:
and may it rest easy over you
when at last you lay out under it:
may it rest so lightly over you,
that your soul may be off from under it quickly
and up and off,
and on its way to God.
And now may the Lord bless you all,
and bless you kindly.

An Irish Blessing

Notes

1. *Seeking*

    1. Nouwen, Henri, *Bread for the Journey*, Darton, Longman and Todd, 1996.
    2. West, Angela, *Deadly Innocence: Feminism and the Mythology of Sin*, Cassell, 1995.

2. *Wonder*

    1. Mayne, Michael, *This Sunrise of Wonder*, Fount, 1995.
    2. MacLeod, George, *The Whole Earth Shall Cry Glory*, Wild Goose Publications, 1985.
    3. Roberts, Elizabeth and Amidon, Elias (eds.), *Earth Prayers*, Harper San Francisco, 1991.
    4. Quoted in Webber, Julian Lloyd (compiler), *Song of the Birds: Sayings, Stories and Impressions of Pablo Casals*, Robson Books, 1985.
    5. Roberts, Elizabeth and Amidon, Elias (eds.), *Earth Prayers*, Harper San Francisco, 1991.

3. *Reawakening to mystery*

    1. From a paper presented at the Orthodox Assembly, Sofia, Bulgaria, *The transfigured creation*, Section III.
    2. Abram, David, *The Spell of the Sensuous*, Vintage Books, 1997.

4. *Befriending the earth*

    1. From an unpublished poem by a friend, Leslie Bates.

Notes

2. From an article by Dean Carter in *Kindred Spirit*, Issue 46, 1999.
3. Roberts, Elizabeth and Amidon, Elias (eds.), *Earth Prayers*, Harper San Francisco, 1991.

5. Listening to the post-modern world

1. Küng, Hans (ed.), *Yes to a Global Ethic*, SCM Press, 1996.
2. From an article by Brendan Walsh in *The Tablet*, March 1996.

6. Reconnecting with our depths

1. Gallagher, Paul, *Clashing Symbols*, Darton, Longman and Todd, 1997.
2. From an article by Paul Vallely in *The Tablet*, 8 May 1999.
3. Hanh, Thich Nhat, *Living Buddha, Living Christ*, Rider, 1996.
4. ibid.

7. Praying

1. White, E., *Songs of God's People*, Oxford University Press, 1988, Hymn No. 89.
2. Camara, Helder, *Hoping Against All Hope*, Orbis Books, 1984.
3. Cassidy, Sheila, *Sharing the Darkness*, Darton, Longman and Todd, 1988.
4. Dalrymple, Jock, *Letting Go in Love*, Darton, Longman and Todd, 1986.

8. Realising God is not always a man!

1. Johnson, Elizabeth A., *She Who Is*, Crossroad 1994.

9. Rediscovering community

1. Küng, Hans, *Global Responsibility*, SCM Press, 1990.
2. Duncan, Geoffrey (ed.), *Wisdom is Calling*, Canterbury Press, Norwich, 1999.

Notes

11. Sharing our stories

1. From an interview with Rabbi Abraham Heschel in *Intellectual Digest*, June 1973, p.78.
2. Neu, Diann, in Roberts, Elizabeth and Amidon, Elias (eds.), *Earth Prayers*, Harper San Francisco, 1991.

13. Basil and Mary's holiness

1. From an article by Patrick Maguire in *The Tablet*, 26 June 1999, p. 886.
2. Tagore, Rabindranath, in Green, Barbara and Gollancz, Victor (eds.), *God of a Hundred Names*, Gollancz, 1985.

15. Antonio's magic

1. Rinpoche, Sogyal, *The Tibetan Book of Living and Dying*, Rider, 1992.
2. Vanier, Jean, *Becoming Human*, Darton, Longman and Todd, 1998.

19. Mahala's gift

1. Cassidy, Sheila, *Sharing the Darkness,* Darton, Longman and Todd, 1988.

21. Sara's justified anger

1. From an article by a member of the Quaker's Women's Group in *Yearly Meeting 1994*, Volume II (London Meeting of the Society of Friends).

22. Phoebe, Anna and Diana's hopes

1. Richards, Mary, *Centering*, Wesleyan University Press, 1974.
2. Willetts, Phoebe, in Guinness, Michele, *Tapestry of Voices*, Triangle, 1996.
3. Eck, Diana, *Encountering God*, Beacon Press, 1993.

Notes

25. Healing

1. Briggs, Anna, in *Songs of God's People*, Oxford University Press, 1988, Hymn No. 113.

26. Accepting life's unfinished symphonies

1. Rolheiser, Ronald, *Seeking Spirituality*, Hodder and Stoughton, 1998.
2. From Keay, Kathy (compiler), *Laughter, Silence and Shouting*, Harper Collins, 1994.

27. Valuing different sexualities

1. Sullivan, Andrew, *Virtually Normal*, Picador, 1995.

29. Dying

1. Cousins, Norman, quoted in Tilleraas, Percy, *The Colour of Light*, Hazelden Foundation, 1988.
2. Quoist, Michel, *Christ is Alive*, Gill and MacMillan, 1971.
3. Nicholl, Donald, *The Testing of Hearts*, Darton, Longman and Todd, 1998.
4. From Appleton, George (ed.), *The Oxford Book of Prayer*, Oxford University Press, 1988.

31. Yearning for justice

1. From Kameeta, Zephania, *Why, O Lord: Psalms and Sermons from Namibia*, World Council of Churches, 1986.

35. Facing up to racism

1. Hope, S. 'Light a candle, don't just curse the dark!', *The Coracle*, April 1999, p. 14.
2. From a prayer used in various liturgies by the World Council of Churches.

38. Remembering

1. Adapted from a prayer by Elie Wiesel and Albert Friedlander

Notes

39. *Reviving radical prophecy*

    1. MacLeod, George, *Only One Way Left*, Iona Community
       Publications, 4th Edition, 1964.
    2. Kameeta, Zephania, *Why, O Lord: Psalms and Sermons
       from Namibia*, World Council of Churches, 1986.
    3. Romero, O. in Edwards, Maureen (ed.), *Living Prayers for
       Today*, International Bible Reading Association, 1996.
    4. From an article by Father Jock Dalrymple in the *Beda
       Review*, March 1985.

40. *Seeking moral imagination*

    1. Richards, Mary, *Centering*, Wesleyan University Press,
       1974.
    2. ibid.

41. *Welcoming the provisional*

    1. Dale, Alan, *New World*, Oxford University Press, 1967.
    2. Leunig, Michael, *A Common Prayer*, Collins Dove, 1990.
    3. Hillesum, E. 'An Interrupted Life' in Harris, Paul (ed.), *The
       Fire of Silence and Stillness*, Darton, Longman and Todd,
       1995.

42. *Building bridges*

    1. Edwards, Maureen (ed.), *Living Prayers for Today*,
       International Bible Reading Association, 1996.
    2. ibid.
    3. ibid.

43. *Giving thanks*

    1. Peterson, Eugene H., *The Message: Psalms*, Navpress,
       Colorado, 1994.

44. *Announcing good news*

    1. Adapted from a section in Buhlmann, Walbert, *With Eyes to
       See: Church and World in the Third Millennium*, St Paul
       Publications, Fowler Wright, 1990.

Notes

46. *Journeying on*

1. Camara, Helder, *A Thousand Reasons for Living*, Darton, Longman and Todd, 1981.

47. *Moving on in the light of God*

1. Tirabassi, Maren C. and Eddy, Kathy Wonson (eds.), *Gifts of Many Cultures: Worship Resources for the Global Community*, United Church Press, 1995.

Further reading

Barbour, Ian, *Religion in an Age of Science*, Harper, 1990.

Bradley, Ian, *Celtic Christianity: Making Myths and Chasing Dreams*, Edinburgh University Press, 1999.

Duncan, Geoffrey (ed.), *Wisdom is Calling: An Anthology of Hope, an Agenda for Change*, Canterbury Press Norwich, 1999.

Eadie, Donald, *Grain in Winter*, Epworth Press, 1999.

Ford, Michael, *Wounded Prophet: A Portrait of Henri Nouwen*, Darton, Longman and Todd, 1999.

Griffiths, Bede, *A New Vision of Reality: Western Science, Eastern Mysticism and Christian Faith*, Fount, 1989.

Guinness, Michele (ed.), *Tapestry of Voices: Meditations on Women's Lives*, Triangle, 1996.

Hall, Stuart (ed.), *Modernity and its Futures: Understanding Modern Societies*, Polity Press, 1996.

Johnson, Elizabeth, *She Who Is: The Mystery of God in Feminist Theological Discourse*, Crossroad, 1994.

Küng, Hans and Schmidt, Helmut (eds.), *A Global Ethic and Global Responsibilities*, SCM Press, 1998.

Leech, Kenneth, *The Sky is Red: Discerning the Signs of the Times*, Darton, Longman and Todd, 1997.

Millar, Peter, *An Iona Prayer Book*, Canterbury Press Norwich, 1998.

Schreiter, Robert, *The New Catholicity: Theology Between the Local and the Global*, Orbis, 1998.

Shanks, Norman, *Iona: God's Energy. The Spirituality and Vision of the Iona Community*, Hodder and Stoughton, 1999.

Vallely, Paul (ed.), *The New Politics: Catholic Social Teaching in the Twenty-First Century*, SCM Press, 1998.

Vanier, Jean, *Becoming Human*, Darton, Longman and Todd, 1998.

the same day they were caught. On 29 July a man was hanged for theft.[28]

Wolfe experienced the brutal realities of North American warfare just days after his pleasant dinner with the French ladies. Tales of fords across the Montmorency had sparked his interest. If these were 'practicable' then he could march across the river and drive the French troops from the Beauport shore altogether. It is easy to see how his frustration with the navy boosted his enthusiasm for finding one of these fords. A straightforward attack across the Montmorency would be an army operation alone. There would be no need for the kind of cooperation with the navy that he obviously found so irksome. On 26 July, therefore, Wolfe set out to look for the ford. Mackellar records that he took 'Brigadier Murray, with Otway's 35th Regiment, five companies of Light Infantry, and one of the Rangers, and two field pieces'. The two cannon were probably six pounders which were more mobile than the heavier pieces. Even so, Mackellar continues, 'after we had gone about a mile and a half the field-pieces were sent back to camp, the road being too bad to get them on'.[29]

It was thick woodland. As they pushed further upstream the roar of the falls grew ever quieter. This was the terrain which suited the Canadians and Native Americans perfectly. The latter's relationship with the French had been strained by their inactivity. Around that time Vaudreuil wrote to de Lévis describing them as 'too lively' and hoping that the latter had found a way to make them 'less impatient'.[30] Now Wolfe was offering a solution. His men had marched well before dawn and in the semi-darkness, at 0400 hours, with the sunrise still an hour away, the sound of muskets and high-pitched war cries heralded a first attack on the column. Wolfe's 'Family Journal' describes it as a 'skirmish with about 20 Indians'.[31] They fell upon the lighter troops who were to the front and flanks of the main column. These light infantrymen and rangers skirmished tenaciously and allowed the march to continue.

The column reached the ford a few hours later. On the far side there was 'a breast work of considerable extent'.[32] Wolfe tried to get a good look at the practicality of crossing it but was forced to stay under cover by a withering fire from the far bank. 'As the river is narrow here,' his 'Family Journal' says, 'the enemy's fire galled our left from their entrenchments.'³³ It was harrowing but worse was to follow. At 0900 hours another attack from across the river threatened to overwhelm Wolfe's column completely.

'A strong body of Indians passed over to attack us,' reported Wolfe's 'Family Journal' and the outcome was 'doubtful for some time'.³⁴ Mackellar estimated that no less than fifteen hundred men now attacked the British. They had crept up the riverbank from a ford higher up and now hurled themselves at a company of light infantry who retreated under the onslaught. The French attack then crashed into two companies of Otway's 35th Regiment. As always this assault relied on speed, surprise, and accuracy with the musket or rifle. These lightning tactics were supposed to spread panic in the enemy and make them scatter, allowing the attackers to hunt down the isolated individuals. The psychological impact was paramount. Against novices these tactics were awesomely effective.

The 35th were no novices. They were no longer the men who, two years before at Fort William Henry, had surrendered to Montcalm's army and naively expected safe passage to the nearest British fort. On that terrible occasion the Native allies of the French, furious that not a scalp had been taken and the enemy were allowed to march away, could not be restrained and had fallen on them. The wounded in the infirmary had been slaughtered and soldiers initially robbed and then beaten and killed. In desperation the British soldiers had offered the Natives their own rum ration, only to fan the flames as the alcohol-crazed attacks became more and more brutal. Even fresh graves were dug up and corpses scalped. French officers had intervened, appalled that the terms of surrender were being broken. Around two hundred men, women, and children were killed, and many others captured. These latter were ransomed and returned to the British by a contrite French colonial administration. Many survivors scattered into the wilderness and stumbled back to British-held territory days later. It was denounced as a war-crime throughout the English speaking world. Now on the banks of the Montmorency the men of the 35th were taking their revenge.

The unit was vastly changed to the one that had arrived in New York in June 1756. The battered and discoloured orange cuffs and